Pinch OF Nom
ALL IN ONE

Pinch OF Nom
ALL IN ONE

ONE-PAN, SLIMMING MEALS

bluebird

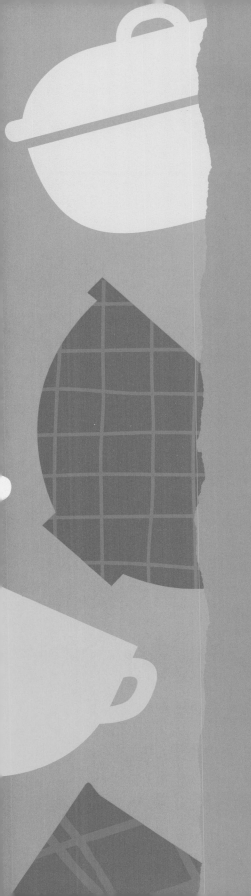

CONTENTS

HELLO

...and welcome!

Let's start with a big HELLO and an even bigger THANK YOU! Each and every time we sit down to write these introductions, it feels just as surreal as the very first time. We'll never get over how lucky we are to bring recipes that we love to cook and eat into your kitchens, and we never take for granted that the incredible Pinch of Nom community is by our side. Simply put, these books couldn't happen without you. We hope this collection of one-pot meals helps to make your life just that little bit easier and a whole lot more delicious!

SO, WHY *ALL IN ONE*?

Can you imagine anything simpler than cooking your ingredients all in one pot, so that your whole meal is ready all at once? Only our easiest, breeziest recipes have made the cut for this book, so you can say goodbye to piles and piles of washing-up, and hello to tasty, slimming-friendly food that's blissfully mess free.

Designed to work in perfect harmony with all the other Pinch of Nom books on your

shelves, we've packed 100 of our ultimate one-pot recipes into this book, so you can flick to a comforting classic or try something new and different, all depending on what you fancy on the day. We know how much you all love your slow cookers, and they're made for one-pot cooking. We've made sure there are plenty of slow cooker recipes tucked away inside this book, so you can put your favourite kitchen gadget to good use on days when you need dinner waiting for you as you walk through the door.

You'll feel right at home when you spot the chapters inside the next few pages – all your old favourites are here! We've made sure you're covered for lunch, dinner and dessert with Soups, Stews & Casseroles, Bakes & Roasts, Fakeaways and Sweet Treats. Whether you're in a time pinch, cooking on a budget, or trying to feed healthy food to your family, we're confident you'll find exactly what you need in All in One.

Along with family favourite traybakes and saucy dishes you can leave to simmer, you'll spot a few unexpected All in One recipes in

these pages too! If you thought you couldn't cook your Sunday dinner without having to deal with a mountain of pots and pans to clean, think again. Turn to page 214 to rustle up our Sunday Roast Chicken Traybake, gorgeous gravy included.

When the takeaway feels like the easiest option, we'd love to tempt you with a warming bowl of Yellow Pea and Sweet Potato Curry instead (page 110). It's mild, fragrant and – you guessed it – all cooked in one single saucepan. Room for pudding? You can't say no to a slice of Triple Chocolate Cake, especially as it's drizzled with a little chocolate syrup (page 237).

We'll stop waffling on now, so you can flick ahead to the good part and start bookmarking all the dishes you'll be trying first! We feel incredibly lucky to be bringing these recipes into your kitchen, and we hope you'll enjoy every single bite.

Kay x Kate

THE FOOD

As a classically trained chef, Kate has always loved recreating dishes and putting an original spin on classic recipes. This is how the very first Pinch of Nom recipes came to be, and it's this passion that means we can continue to bring fresh new flavours to you today. Kate and her small team love nothing more than getting into the kitchen and experimenting with ingredients until some Pinch of Nom magic is created!

Along with being effortless to prepare and leaving behind minimal washing up, cooking meals all in one pot can save time, energy and be better for your budget too. That said, it was a no-brainer to make All in One the theme of this book. Just like all of our recipes, we've built these dishes around our motto of 'less fuss, more flavour' – so you'll find that we stick to simple, easy-to-find ingredients that you can use to make multiple meals.

A whopping 91 of the 100 recipes you'll find in the next few chapters are brand new and exclusive to this book. You'll spot that we've also added in 9 much-loved one-pot wonders from our website too, so if you prefer to have your favourites at your fingertips (rather than on a screen), you're in luck!

Our recipes are designed to suit any level of cooking skill, and All in One dishes in particular are great for beginners. If you've cooked from any of our previous books, you'll know we're all about simple, easy-to-follow methods. Plus, if something can be cooked in more than one way, we'll give you the option, with an alternative method included.

We always try to create recipes that everyone can enjoy, so keep an eye out for where we've flagged vegetarian, vegan, gluten-free or dairy-free recipes. As well as being slimming friendly and completely delicious, the ultimate aim of the food in this cookbook is to fill your plate with meals you enjoy cooking, and can't wait to eat. We hope each time you rustle up one of our tasty traybakes, comforting casseroles or slow-cooker stews, you'll agree that it was easy to make, and even easier to clean up!

RECIPE TAGS

EVERYDAY LIGHT

These recipes can be used freely throughout the week. All the meals, including accompaniments, are under 400 calories. Or, in the case of sweet treats, under 200 calories. Of course, if you're counting calories, you still need to keep an eye on the values, but these recipes should help you stay under your allowance.

WEEKLY INDULGENCE

These recipes are still low in calories, at between 400 and 500 calories, or 200-300 for sweet treats, but should be saved for once or twice a week. Mix them into your Everyday Light recipes for variety.

SPECIAL OCCASION

These recipes are often lower in calories than their full-fat counterparts, but they need to be saved for a special occasion. This tag indicates any main meals that are over 500 calories, or over 300 for sweet treats.

KCAL and CARB VALUES

All of our recipes have been worked out as complete meals, using standardised portion sizes for any accompaniments, as advised by the British Nutrition Foundation. Carb values are included for those who need to measure their intake.

GLUTEN-FREE RECIPES

We have marked gluten-free recipes with a GF icon. All these recipes are either free of gluten or we have suggested gluten-free ingredient swaps of common ingredients, such as stock cubes and Worcestershire sauce. Please check labelling to ensure the product you buy is gluten free.

FREEZABLE RECIPES

Look out for the 'Freezable' icon to indicate freezer-friendly dishes. The icon applies to the main dish only, not the suggested accompaniments.

STANDARD FREEZING *and* REHEATING GUIDELINES

For most recipes, you'll be able to follow our standard freezing and reheating guidelines below (we'll let you know if a recipe requires more specific instructions):

· Allow food to cool and then freeze as soon as it is cold enough.
· Place in a container or bag that is suitable for freezing.
· Add a label telling you the name of the recipe and the date you're freezing it

The general consensus is that you can keep food frozen for around 6 months, although after 3 it'll start to lose its flavour.

You should reheat and eat defrosted food within 24 hours. Please don't reheat frozen food until it has defrosted thoroughly in a fridge or microwave. NHS guidelines (correct at the time of writing) state that you should reheat food until it reaches 75°C/167°F and holds that temperature for 2 minutes. Always make sure it's piping hot throughout (you should stir while reheating to ensure this).

Keep cooked rice in the fridge no longer than 1 day before reheating it, or you can freeze it and defrost thoroughly in the fridge before reheating. Always make sure you reheat rice until it is piping hot, and never reheat it more than once.

If you're ever unsure about freezing and reheating a recipe safely, we'd strongly advise referring to the official NHS guidelines.

All of these calculations and dietary indicators are for guidance only and are not to be taken as complete fact without checking ingredients and product labelling yourself.

BATCH COOKING

If this isn't your first Pinch of Nom book, you probably already know how much we love to batch cook! Whether you prefer to go all out and meal prep for the whole week, or just like to have leftovers for an easy-peasy lunch option, we're here to help you make your food go further. The great thing about All in One recipes (aside from having fewer pots to clean) is that they're generally ideal for batch-cooking. This book is full of hearty soups, stews and traybakes that reheat like a dream – and many of the dishes taste even better after a day in the fridge! Flick to page 54 and double up the portions of our Harissa Beef Stew – trust us, you'll thank us later when you've got spare servings stashed away. As always, we've included specific refrigerating and freezing instructions on each freezer-friendly recipe, but please make sure you familiarise yourself with the latest NHS food safety guidelines before you get started. To kick things off, we've detailed a few tried-and-trusted house rules for you below (all information is correct at the time of writing).

MAKE ROOM FOR LEFTOVERS

It's a good idea to check you've got space in your fridge or freezer before you start cooking. You don't want leftovers going to waste!

DIVIDE INTO PORTIONS

Store leftovers in individual-sized servings – your food will cool, freeze and defrost loads quicker when you portion it out. Plus, it makes it so much easier when you want to grab leftovers for a one-person lunch or dinner!

USE AIRTIGHT CONTAINERS *and* FREEZER BAGS

Storing food correctly is the key to keeping leftovers fresh for longer. Whether you use containers or bags, make sure they seal properly to avoid 'freezer burn' (uninvited air damaging your food). Containers that are also microwave-safe are the best investment, as there's no need to buy separate ones for the sake of reheating.

USE REFRIGERATED FOODS WITHIN 2-3 DAYS

Lots of our All in One recipes will taste even better after 24 hours in the fridge, when all the flavours have had more time to develop. You'll just need to keep an eye on how long you store cooked food in the fridge, using leftovers within 2–3 days to avoid the risk of food poisoning. If you'd like to keep leftovers for longer, make sure you freeze them as soon as possible after cooking and cooling.

PUT A LABEL ON IT

You can freeze food for 3–6 months, so it's important to add a freezer-proof label that includes the date on which the meal was cooked. If you're stocking up the freezer for busy days, it's a good idea to also add the name of the recipe, and organise your freezer drawer so that older portions are easy to grab and use up first. Depending on the recipe, some food can be stored beyond 6 months and still be safe to eat, although it might start to lose flavour.

DEFROST THOROUGHLY

Please take care not to reheat food until it has defrosted thoroughly in the fridge or microwave.

REHEAT *and* EAT WITHIN 24 HOURS

NHS guidelines (correct at the time of writing) state that you should reheat food until it reaches 75°C/167°F and holds that temperature for 2 minutes. Stir while reheating, and make sure it's piping hot throughout. You should only ever reheat food once.

STORING RICE

All in One dishes that contain rice are safe to freeze and reheat, but only if they're stored in the right way. Cool the food as quickly as possible (ideally within 1 hour) by putting it in a wide, shallow container. The longer rice is left at room temperature, the greater the risk that it could grow harmful bacteria. Keep cooked rice dishes in the fridge no longer than 1 day before reheating them, or you can freeze and defrost thoroughly in the fridge before reheating. Always make sure you reheat rice until it is piping hot, and never reheat it more than once.

KEY INGREDIENTS

PROTEIN

Fish and lean meats are a great source of protein, providing essential nutrients and keeping you feeling full between meals. In many of our recipes you'll find that you can switch the type of protein for any meat that you prefer, or that suits your budget better. This especially applies to any mince recipes; turkey, beef or pork mince are easily interchangeable. In all cases where meat is used in this book, we'd recommend using the leanest possible cuts and trimming off all visible fat. And don't forget, vegetarian protein options can always be used instead of meat in all of the recipes in this book.

HERBS *and* SPICES

Herbs and spices keep your food interesting without adding lots of extra calories. We've used inexpensive dried ingredients where possible, with fresh ingredients only where they're necessary to get the flavour of a dish just right. Don't be shy with spices – not all of them burn your mouth off! We've added a spice-level icon to the recipes in this book, so you know what to expect. Always taste your food before adding extra spicing; this is particularly important if you're planning to double the quantities of sauce in a recipe. You'll often find that you don't need to double the amount of all the ingredients to achieve the right flavour – spices, vinegars, mustard and hot sauces should be added gradually, to taste.

STOCKS, SAUCE *and* THICKENERS

When you remove fat from a dish, flavours can dwindle. Adding spices is one way to boost flavours, but often the level of acidity in a recipe is much more important. When it comes to balancing and boosting flavours in our dishes, we love to use vinegar, soy sauce, fish sauce, Worcestershire sauce or Henderson's relish. One of Pinch of Nom's essential ingredients is the humble stock cube or stock pot; they add instant flavour and they're so versatile. We use various flavoured stock cubes and pots throughout this book, but there's always an option if you can't get your hands on the exact ones we've used. White wine stock pots, for example, can be tricky to find, but you can use 100ml of dry white wine and reduce the amount of water used in the recipe by 100ml instead (bear in mind this will add extra calories). It's worth noting that sauces, stock cubes and pots are often high in salt, so you may want to swap for reduced-salt versions.

We're often asked for tips on how to thicken soups, sauces and gravies. In the pre-slimming days, we wouldn't have thought twice about using a few tablespoons of flour to thicken liquids. Nowadays we're always on the lookout

for lower-calorie and gluten-free options. Letting liquids reduce is a good way of thickening sauces without adding anything extra. As the moisture evaporates, the flavours get more concentrated too, so the end result will taste even better.

You can also thicken recipes with potatoes (yes, really!). They're super starchy so they can be blitzed or mashed into your sauce or soup to soak up extra liquid. Bear in mind that this method will add some extra calories (1 large potato, approx. 370g is about 311 kcal).

A tomato-based dish such as tomato soup or Bolognese can be thickened slightly using some tomato puree. This will add about 50 kcal per 50g tablespoon.

You can use egg yolks or whole beaten eggs to thicken some soups and sauces. Drizzle a little of the hot liquid onto the egg, whisking vigorously, then stir the egg into the pan and heat gently until it thickens. 1 medium (57g) egg is about 76 kcal and 1 medium (18g) egg yolk is about 55 kcal.

If making a roux-style sauce you can cut down on calories by making a slurry rather than using loads of butter. Simply mix your measured-out flour with a little water, then stir it into boiling liquid and simmer for a few minutes to cook the flour. 1 level tablespoon (20g) of plain flour is about 71 kcal. Another instant way to thicken any mixture is by using cornflour. This needs to be made into a slurry by adding a little cold water and then adding to the boiling liquid. Be sure to cook it until the starchy taste has gone. 1 level tablespoon of cornflour (20g) is about 69 kcal.

It can be tempting to thicken stews or chillies with gravy granules, but this can add quite a few calories if you have a heavy hand. 1 teaspoon (5g) of gravy granules is about 21 kcal (depending on the brand). It's worth bearing in mind that gravy granules can also be high in salt.

LEMONS *and* LIMES

Lemons and limes pack a punch when it comes to flavour, and they're often used in both sweet and savoury cooking. We love a light, lemony dessert like the zesty Lemon Posset you'll find on page 252. Using bottled lemon and lime juice can be more cost effective – just be sure to refrigerate them once opened.

REDUCED-FAT DAIRY

Substituting high-fat dairy products with clever alternatives can make a dish instantly lower in calories. You'll find that we'll often use reduced-fat cream cheese or spreadable cheese rather than the higher-fat versions. The same applies to any recipes that may traditionally contain heavy, high-calorie cream. We have swapped this out for a light double cream alternative such as Elmlea.

PLANT-BASED ALTERNATIVES

We often use plant-based alternatives to dairy milk because they're low in fat and bring added flavour to a dish. Coconut plant-based drinks are a great substitute for high-fat tinned coconut milk, and almond milk adds a lovely nutty flavour when it's added into recipes. Make sure you pick up the unsweetened coconut or almond milk alternatives rather than any tinned versions; these will normally be found in a carton container. If you plan on making vegan recipes, you can always swap meat for plant-based tofu. Generally you'll want to make sure you buy the extra-firm variety, and follow our instructions on the Thai-Style Basil Tofu Stir Fry recipe (page 126) carefully to learn how to press it before cooking – you'll want to get rid of as much excess liquid as possible to get the best finished results.

TINS

Don't be afraid to bulk-buy tinned essentials! Beans, tomatoes, lentils, sweetcorn, potatoes and tuna all come in handy time and time again. We often use them to add texture and flavour to stews, soups and salads. Using tinned ingredients can really help to keep costs down, and you'll never know the difference – used in these sorts of recipes they'll taste just as good as their fresh counterparts. Keep an eye out for tinned apricots; they're a little more out of the ordinary.

FROZEN FRUIT *and* VEG

Frozen fruit and veg make great filler ingredients and are perfect low-cost alternatives for recipes such as stews, where fresh ingredients aren't always necessary. Most of the time they're already peeled and chopped too, so they save time as well as money; you can just throw them in alongside your other ingredients.

PULSES, RICE *and* BEANS

High in both protein and fibre, keeping a few tinned or dried mixed beans and pulses in the cupboard is never going to do any harm! They're especially tasty in stews, soups and curries. Grains like pearl barley, quinoa, bulgar wheat are ideal when it comes to one-pot cooking. They'll cook in sauces or stock, and add filling-power to keep you satisfied between meals.

BREAD

A great source of fibre, wholemeal bread is filling and versatile too. We often use gluten-free breads as they tend to contain fewer calories and less sugar, making them an easy swap when you want to shave off a few calories.

PASTA, NOODLES *and* RICE

Forget setting another pan to boil – we've added the side dish into the same pot for lots of these recipes! Packets of microwavable rice are great to have in the cupboard, especially when you don't have time to wait for your grains to boil: fluffy perfection, in seconds! Straight to wok noodles are also a game-changer when it comes to *All in One* cooking. Pop them right into the pan and sizzle them along with the rest of your ingredients. Adding pasta into your meal will instantly make it nice and filling – most of the time any shape will do, but orzo and giant couscous are ideal for one-pot dishes since the individual pieces cook quickly. Potato-based gnocchi also appears in this book, and it's usually readily available in the supermarkets.

EGGS

Eggs are protein rich, tasty and versatile! The humble egg can be used in so many different ways, from baking and binding ingredients together, through to making our hearty Pea, Potato and Onion Frittata (page 189).

LOW-CALORIE COOKING SPRAY

One of the best ways to cut down on cooking with oils and fats is to use a low-calorie cooking spray. A spritz of this will make little difference to the end result of your food, but it can make a huge difference to the calories consumed.

READY-MADE PASTRY

There's no need to become a pastry chef overnight – just buy it ready-made! Not only can you usually find a light version with reduced calories, it saves so much time and hassle when making our Pizza Tart (page 208).

SWEETENER

There are so many sweeteners out there, it can be tricky to know which is the best substitute for regular sugar. Sweeteners vary in sweetness and swapping them weight-for-weight with regular sugar can give you different results. In our recipes we use granulated sweetener, not powdered sweetener, as it has larger 'crystals'. This can be used weight-for-weight anywhere that you're replacing sugar.

OUR FAVOURITE KIT

NON-STICK PANS

If there's one bit of kit that Pinch of Nom would advise as an investment kitchen piece, it would be a decent set of non-stick pans. The better the non-stick quality of your pans, the fewer cooking oils and fats you'll need to use in order to stop food sticking and burning. For many of the recipes in this book we'd recommend picking up a large, deep frying pan with a lid, that's suitable for using both on the hob and in the oven. You'll also find that a large non-stick wok or frying pan will come in handy time and time again. Keep your pans in good health by cleaning them properly and gently with soapy water.

MIXING BOWLS

A couple of mixing bowls will see you through most kinds of recipes. Smaller bowls give you more control when you're whisking ingredients and larger bowls mean more room to mix it up.

KITCHEN KNIVES

Every kitchen needs a good set of knives. If you can, invest in some good quality, super-sharp knives – blunt knives have a habit of bouncing off ingredients, which can make them more dangerous than sharper ones. You'll need to mind your fingers with super-sharp knives too, but you'll be glad you invested when you've got knives that glide through veg, saving you so much time and effort.

KNIFE SHARPENER

Once you've invested in your sharp knives, you'll want to keep them that way! Keep them nice and sharp so you can carry on slicing and dicing like a pro.

CHOPPING BOARDS

As well as protecting your surfaces, a good set of chopping boards are the key to a safe and hygienic kitchen. We'd suggest picking up a full set of colour-coordinated chopping boards, with separate boards for veg, meat, fish and dairy. They'll make it so much easier to keep your ingredients separate, and most sets are easy to clean and tidy away once your meal prep is sorted.

FOOD PROCESSOR / BLENDER / STICK BLENDER

These are essential pieces of kit for a lot of Pinch of Nom recipes. We like to make sauces from scratch, so a decent blender or food processor is a lifesaver. A stick blender can be used on most occasions if you're looking for something cheaper or more compact. It's well worth the investment for the flavour of all those homemade sauces.

FREEZABLE TUBS

Most of the recipes in this book are freezable and ideal for batch cooking. It's a good idea to invest in some freezer-proof tubs – and they don't have to be plastic. For a more eco-friendly solution, choose glass storage containers; just remember to check they're freezer-safe.

*Note on plastic: We have made a conscious effort to reduce the amount of non-reusable plastic such as cling film when making our recipes. There are great alternatives to cling film now available, such as silicone stretch lids, beeswax food covers, fabric food covers and biodegradable food and freezer bags.

RAMEKIN DISHES

One of the best ways to handle portion control on sweet treats or desserts is to serve up your puddings in individual portions. By making dishes in small ramekins, you not only give yourself a set portion (which makes calorie counting so much easier), but it also makes the food look super faaaaancy!

OVENWARE

For many of these All in One recipes you'll need either an oven tray, roasting tin or casserole dish. We'd recommend choosing casserole dishes that can be used both on the hob and in the oven. A good set of basics would include a medium and a large deep casserole dish with lid, along with a large shallow casserole dish with lid. Keep your ovenware in tip top condition for longer by lining them with non-stick baking paper before cooking. If a specific size of dish is essential to the success of a recipe, we've listed this as 'Special Equipment'.

HOB

We cook on an induction hob. If you have a ceramic/hot-plate hob you may have to cook dishes for a little longer.

FINE GRATER

Using a fine grater is one of those surprising revelations. You won't believe the difference between grating cheese with a fine grater versus a standard grater. 45g of cheese, for example, can easily cover an oven dish when using a fine grater. You can also use it for citrus zest, garlic and ginger – it helps a little go a long, long way.

GARLIC CRUSHER

You'll never miss the faff of finely chopping garlic once you've invested in a garlic crusher. Relatively cheap to pick up, you won't go back after you've squeezed that first clove into a perfect paste. It'll save you so much time and it helps your garlic spread evenly throughout the dish.

MEASURING SPOONS

Want to make sure you never get muddled between a tsp and tbsp? Pinch of Nom has absolutely, definitely never made this mistake. Honest. But these days we're never without a trusty set of measuring spoons, which help make sure it's not a tablespoon of chilli when it should have been a teaspoon. Just make sure you use a butter knife to level off the spoon – you'll be surprised how much extra you add when the spoonful is heaped.

HEATPROOF JUG

A measuring jug is essential for measuring out wet ingredients. We recommend getting a heatproof version that you can stick in the microwave when needed.

UTENSILS

You'll find various bits and bobs used in these recipes, many of which you probably already have in your kitchen. As a good starting point, we'd recommend making sure you have a pair of sharp kitchen scissors, a fish slice, ladle, sieve, pastry brush, large metal spoon, cooling rack and a veg peeler. These are all fairly inexpensive items, but they make a big difference when a recipe calls for something specific.

KITCHEN KIT (THAT'S NICE TO HAVE)

SLOW COOKER

We're big fans of slow cookers, and they're ideal for one-pot cooking. Throw in some ingredients, go out, enjoy your day and return to a home-cooked meal, ready and waiting for you. They're available at a whole range of different price points, and they can end up saving you a lot of time. We use a 3.5 litre slow cooker – please don't attempt to make dishes in a slow cooker any smaller than this.

ELECTRIC PRESSURE COOKER

A pressure cooker is a great investment if you're looking to save time. The high-pressure cooking process creates perfectly tender meat and makes stews taste as though they've been bubbling away for hours. We recommend electric models for safety and ease of use.

ELECTRIC WHISK

No one minds a bit of elbow grease from time to time, but when you're trying to whisk up a storm in the kitchen, it's not cheating to reach for this handy bit of kit. An electric whisk isn't essential, although it's well worth the investment. You'll often find Pinch of Nom dessert recipes recommend using one to whisk plenty of air into fluffy, light desserts.

SOUPS

BUTTERNUT SQUASH *and* ROCKET SOUP

🕐 **10 MINS**   🍲 **1 HR**   ✕ **SERVES 6**

PER SERVING:
105 KCAL /11G CARBS

SPECIAL EQUIPMENT
**Large casserole dish suitable
for oven and hob
Stick blender or food
processor**

low-calorie cooking spray
1 butternut squash, peeled,
    halved and seeds removed
    (about 600g prepped weight)
3 garlic cloves, unpeeled
1 medium red onion, peeled
    and sliced
400ml boiling water
30g rocket
50g dairy-free feta-style
    cheese
20g pecan nuts, chopped

FOR THE SPICE MIX
½ tsp onion powder
½ tsp garlic granules
½ tsp dried mixed herbs
½ tsp medium chilli powder
¼ tsp salt
¼ tsp freshly ground black
    pepper

TO ACCOMPANY
60g wholemeal bread roll
    (+ 146 kcal per roll)

TIP:

We think it's easier
to peel the butternut squash
before you slice it in half. Just
use a normal vegetable peeler!

If you're looking for lunch ideas, you can stop right here! There's nothing better than a bowl of this thick, creamy Butternut Squash and Rocket Soup, especially on a chilly afternoon. To make sure everyone can enjoy these sweet, warming flavours, we've used a dairy-free, vegan-friendly feta-style cheese (although you can use a dairy version if you prefer).

Everyday Light ―――――――――――

Preheat the oven to 220°C (fan 200°C/gas mark 7) and spray a large casserole dish with low-calorie cooking spray.

Combine the spice mix ingredients in a small bowl.

Spray the squash halves with low-calorie cooking spray and coat the butternut squash in the spice mix (you might find it easier to use your hands to rub the spices into the surface of the squash). Add the squash to the casserole dish along with the garlic. Roast in the oven for 45 minutes.

Remove the casserole dish from the oven and add the sliced onion around the squash, then return the dish to the oven for a further 15 minutes. The butternut squash should be soft and the onions beginning to go crispy.

Once cooked, remove the dish from the oven and carefully place on the hob. Squeeze the roasted garlic, discarding the skin. Pour in the boiling water, place over a medium heat and bring to the boil. Remove from the heat and add the rocket and feta-style cheese. Blitz with a stick blender until smooth (or use a food processor), taking care not to splash yourself with hot soup. You may need to add a little more water if it is too thick for your taste. Serve the soup with wholemeal bread rolls.

The soup will keep in the fridge for up to 2 days.

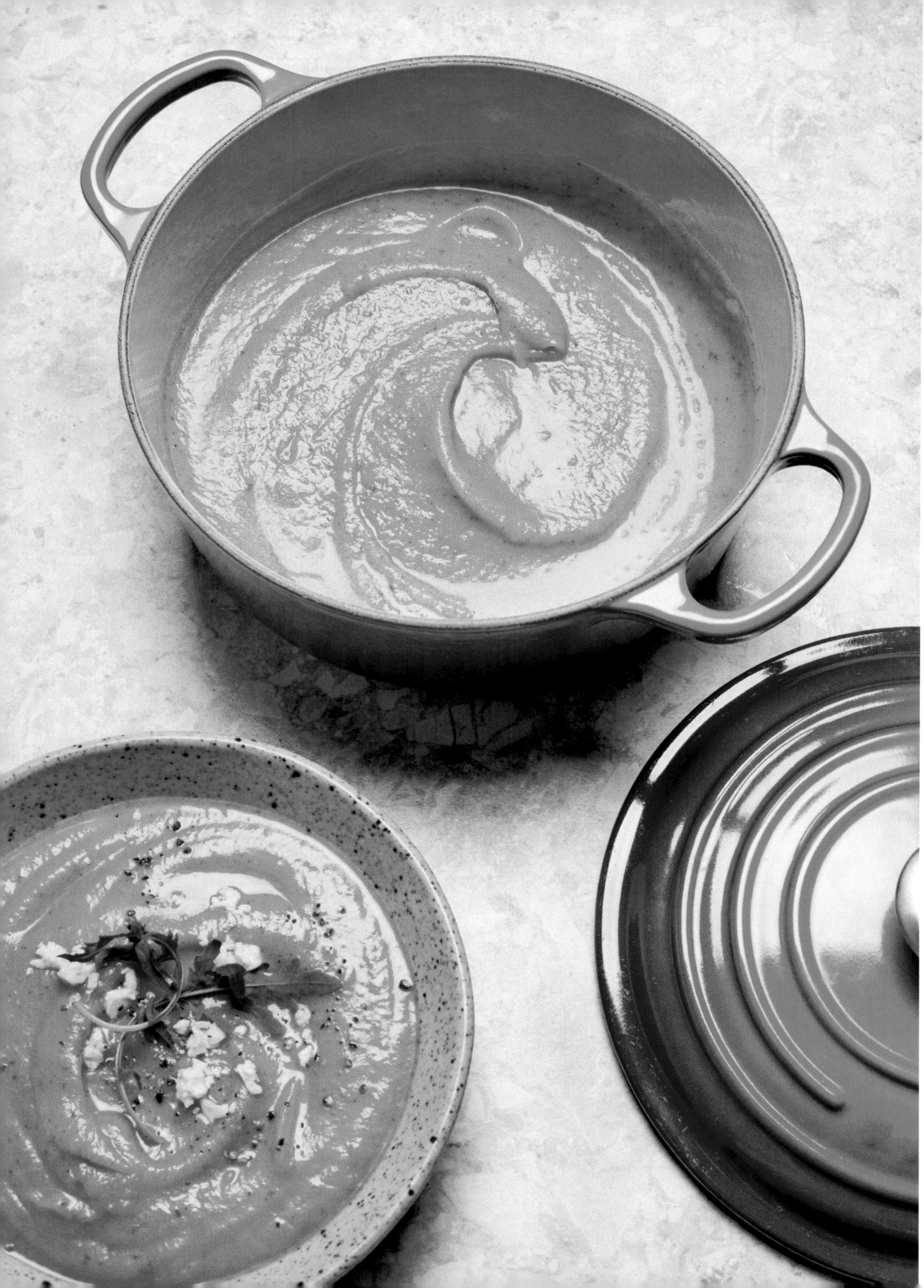

VEGGIE

USE VEGGIE
STOCK CUBE,
OMIT THE
BACON

VEGAN

USE VEGGIE
STOCK
CUBE, OMIT
THE BACON
AND USE DF
YOGHURT

**FREEZE
ME**

WITHOUT THE
YOGHURT AND
DILL GARNISH

**BATCH
COOK**

**DAIRY
FREE**

USE DF
YOGHURT

**GLUTEN
FREE**

USE GF
STOCK CUBE

UKRAINIAN-STYLE BORSCHT

🕐 **20 MINS**　🍲 **45 MINS**　✕ **SERVES 6**

PER SERVING:
191 KCAL / 29G CARBS

low-calorie cooking spray
1 medium onion, peeled and diced
2 garlic cloves, peeled and crushed
1 celery stick, finely chopped
½ small white cabbage, finely shredded
4 smoked bacon medallions, cut into 1cm (½in) dice
1 x 400g tin chopped tomatoes
1 tbsp tomato puree
1 litre chicken stock (1 chicken stock cube dissolved in 1 litre boiling water)
500g cooked fresh peeled beetroot, half coarsely grated and half cut into 1cm (½in) dice
2 medium carrots, peeled and coarsely grated
250g floury potatoes, peeled and cut into 1cm (½in) dice
2 dried bay leaves
1 tbsp cider vinegar
1 tsp white granulated sweetener or granulated sugar
2 tbsp chopped fresh dill, plus extra fronds to serve (*optional*)
sea salt and freshly ground black pepper

TO ACCOMPANY (*optional*)
1 tbsp (45g) fat-free natural yoghurt (+ 25 kcal per tablespoon) and 60g wholemeal bread roll (+ 146 kcal per roll) (+ 171 kcal total per serving)

The national dish of Ukraine, borscht is a hearty soup that gets its distinctive ruby red colour and earthy taste from fresh beetroot. Families often have their own recipe, passed down from generation to generation. For our slimming-friendly take on this classic dish, we use bacon, potatoes and plenty of veggies to complement the beetroot. A splash of vinegar adds a little acidity, which is beautifully balanced by a little sweetener or sugar. Stir in dill and yoghurt just before serving and enjoy!

Everyday Light —————————————————

Spray a large saucepan with low-calorie cooking spray and place over a medium heat. Add the onion, garlic, celery and cabbage and cook for 10 minutes, until softening, then add the bacon and cook for a further 4–5 minutes, until the bacon is cooked. Add the tomatoes, tomato puree, stock, beetroot (grated and diced), carrots, potatoes and bay leaves. Stir well and bring to the boil, then cover, lower the heat and simmer for 25–30 minutes, until the potatoes are soft, stirring occasionally.

Add the vinegar, sweetener or sugar, chopped dill and stir in. Remove the bay leaves and season to taste with salt and pepper.

Serve each portion topped with 1 tablespoon of yoghurt and a sprig of fresh dill (optional).

The soup will keep in the fridge for up to 3 days.

TIPS:

Use fresh cooked peeled beetroot, not pickled beetroot in vinegar which may make the soup too acidic.

Fresh cooked peeled beetroot can be found in supermarkets in 500g vacuum packs.

It's well worth using fresh dill as it adds an authentic, distinctive flavour.

Use a good-quality white granulated sweetener that has the same weight, texture and sweetness as sugar and no aftertaste.

SOUPS

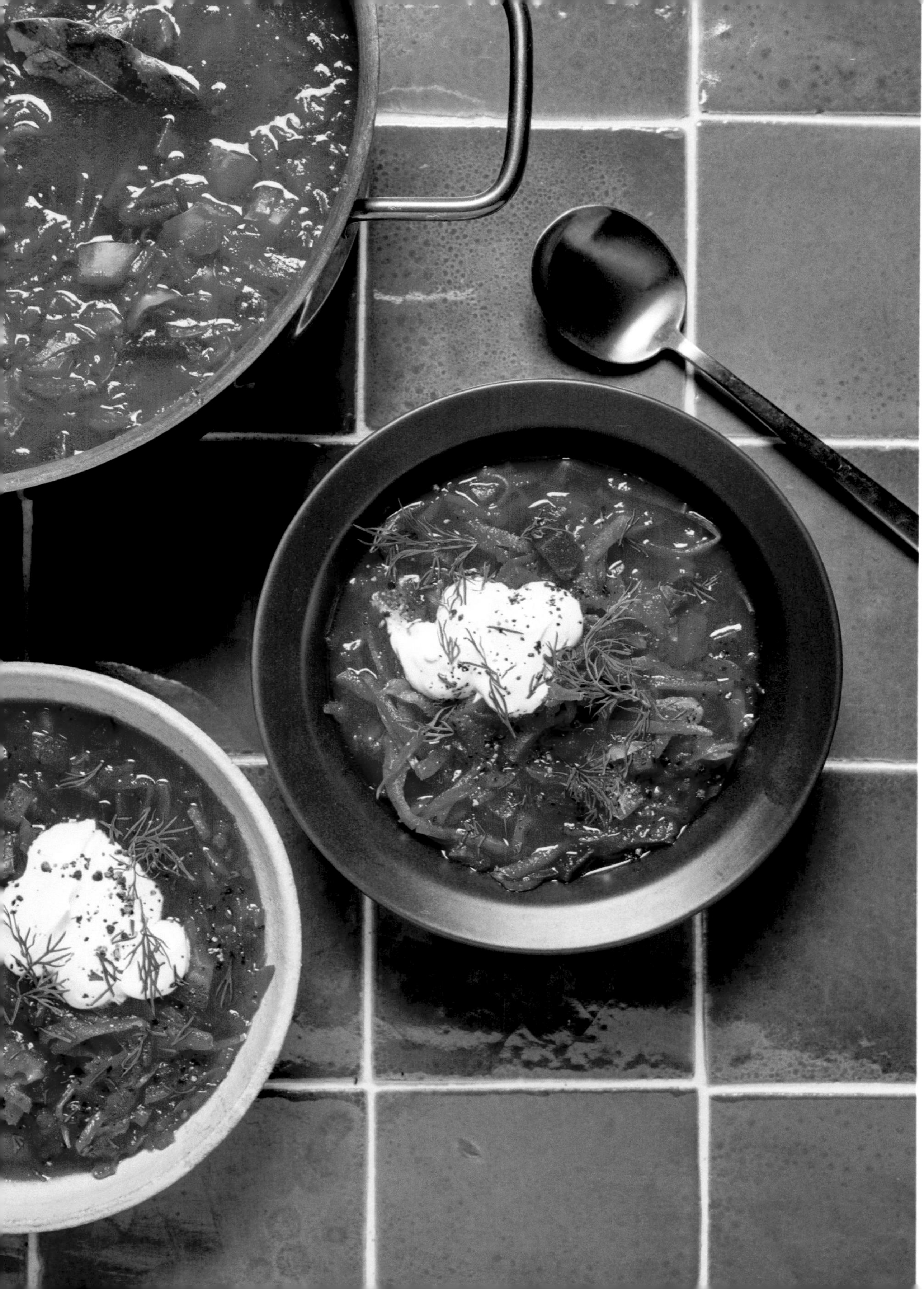

VEGGIE

VEGAN

FREEZE
ME

BATCH
COOK

DAIRY
FREE

GLUTEN
FREE

USE GF
STOCK CUBE

CARROT *and* LENTIL SOUP

🕐 **15 MINS** 🍲 **25 MINS** ✕ **SERVES 6**

PER SERVING:
93 KCAL /12G CARBS

SPECIAL EQUIPMENT
Stick blender or food processor

low-calorie cooking spray
1 medium onion, peeled and diced
3 garlic cloves, peeled and crushed
350g carrots, peeled and sliced
1 x 400g tin green lentils in water, drained
800ml vegetable stock (1 vegetable stock cube dissolved in 800ml boiling water)
3 tbsp mild harissa paste
1 tbsp tomato puree
1 tsp ground cumin
1 tsp sweet smoked paprika
sea salt and freshly ground black pepper

TO ACCOMPANY *(optional)*
60g wholemeal bread roll (+ 146 kcal per roll)

If you need warming up, this is the soup for the job. A hug in a bowl, our velvety blend of carrots and lentils is packed with protein and vitamin C, so every spoonful is brimming with veggie goodness. A sprinkle of smoked paprika and a good dollop of harissa paste are key to unlocking the sumptuous, smoky flavours as this soup simmers away. Our recipe makes 6 hearty portions, but it's always a good idea to make extra and freeze the leftovers for ready-to-reheat lunches on busy days.

Everyday Light

Spray a saucepan with low-calorie cooking spray and place over a medium heat. Add the onion and garlic and cook for 5 minutes, until starting to soften, then add the carrots, lentils, vegetable stock, harissa paste, tomato puree, cumin and paprika to the saucepan and stir well. Bring to the boil, then lower the heat, cover and simmer for 20 minutes, or until the vegetables are soft.

Remove from the heat and blitz the soup until smooth, using a stick blender or food processor, taking care not to splash yourself with hot soup. You may need to do this in batches depending on the size of your food processor. Season to taste with salt and pepper.

Serve the soup with a wholemeal bread roll or other accompaniment of your choice.

The soup will keep in the fridge for up to 3 days.

MOROCCAN-STYLE SOUP

⏱ **15 MINS**　🍲 **1 HR 5 MINS**　✕ **SERVES 6**

VEGGIE

VEGAN

FREEZE ME

BATCH COOK

DAIRY FREE

GLUTEN FREE

USE GF STOCK CUBE

PER SERVING:
156 KCAL /23G CARBS

low-calorie cooking spray
1 medium onion, peeled and
　finely chopped
1 celery stick, finely chopped
1 medium carrot, peeled
　and finely chopped
3 garlic cloves, peeled
　and crushed
1 tsp ground cumin
1 tsp ground turmeric
½ tsp ground cinnamon
½ tsp ground ginger
small pinch of cayenne pepper
1 x 400g tin chopped tomatoes
1 x 400g tin chickpeas in water,
　drained and rinsed
1 x 400g tin brown lentils in
　water, drained and rinsed
3 tbsp tomato puree
1.2 litres vegetable stock
　(1 vegetable stock cube
　dissolved in 1.2 litres
　boiling water)
50g raw basmati rice
handful of curly parsley,
　chopped
handful of fresh coriander
　leaves, chopped
sea salt and freshly ground
　black pepper
1 lemon, cut into 6 wedges,
　to serve

TO ACCOMPANY (optional)
60g wholemeal bread roll
　(+ 146 kcal per roll)

A well-stocked store cupboard will come in really useful for this filling, fragrant soup. Adding tinned tomatoes, chickpeas, lentils and some basmati rice into our mildly-spiced broth helps keep costs down, while making sure you'll feel nice and satisfied when you get to the bottom of your bowlful. Aromatic spices like cumin, ginger, turmeric and cayenne pepper give this dish a North African-style warming flavour, and you won't want to miss out the fresh herbs and squeeze of lemon added right before serving.

Everyday Light

Spray a large saucepan with low-calorie cooking spray and place over a medium heat. Add the onion, celery and carrot and cook for 5–10 minutes, until softening and golden. Lower the heat and add the garlic, cumin, turmeric, cinnamon, ginger and cayenne pepper. Stir well and cook gently for 1–2 minutes to release the fragrant aromas. Take care not to burn the garlic and spices.

Add the chopped tomatoes, chickpeas, lentils, tomato puree and stock and stir well. Bring to the boil, then lower the heat, cover and simmer gently for 35–40 minutes, until all the vegetables are soft.

Stir in the rice, cover and simmer gently for a further 10–15 minutes, or until the rice is cooked and the soup has thickened a little. Stir in the parsley and coriander and season well with salt and pepper, to taste. Squeeze a lemon wedge over each serving of soup and serve with a wholemeal bread roll.

The soup will keep in the fridge for 1 day.

TIPS:

Make sure to use good-quality tinned chopped tomatoes to give the soup a good flavour. Some cheaper brands can be a bit acidic.

This soup has a mild, warming heat. If you would like it hotter, just add a little more cayenne pepper.

This soup is suitable for vegetarians and vegans, but if you are a meat eater you could try adding some meat of your choice.

FREEZE
ME

DAIRY
FREE

OMIT CRÈME
FRAÎCHE
AND ADJUST
CALORIES

GLUTEN
FREE

USE GF STOCK
CUBE

CREAMY BEAN SOUP

🕐 **10 MINS**   🍲 **45 MINS**   ✕ **SERVES 6**

PER SERVING:
158KCAL /15G CARBS

SPECIAL EQUIPMENT
**Stick blender or food
processor**

low-calorie cooking spray
1 onion, peeled and chopped
1 leek, dark green leaves
    removed, chopped
4 smoked bacon medallions,
    diced
4 garlic cloves, peeled and
    crushed
1 tsp dried Italian herbs
1 litre vegetable stock
    (1 vegetable stock cube
    dissolved in 1 litre
    boiling water)
2 x 400g tins cannellini beans in
    water, drained and rinsed
1 tsp white wine vinegar
75g half-fat crème fraîche
small handful of flat-leaf
    parsley, chopped
sea salt and freshly ground
    black pepper

TO ACCOMPANY *(optional)*
60g wholemeal bread roll
    (+ 146 kcal per roll)

Cannellini beans are the star of the show in this herby, garlicky soup. The store-cupboard staple makes the mixture delightfully smooth and silky, and we've ramped up the indulgence even further with a generous dollop of half-fat crème fraîche. You only need a few ingredients and a spare 10 minutes to do the easy prep work. Before you know it, you'll be cooking up enough batches to nourish you for a few days (or longer, if you're freezing them!).

Everyday Light

Spray a large saucepan with low-calorie cooking spray and place over a medium-low heat. Add the onion, leek and bacon and fry for 10–12 minutes, until the vegetables are soft but not browned. Add the garlic and Italian herbs and cook for another minute until fragrant, then add the stock and beans and bring to the boil. Cover with a lid, reduce the heat and simmer for 30 minutes, until the vegetables are cooked through.

Remove from the heat and blitz using a stick blender or do this in a food processor. You can blitz it until completely smooth, or leave some chunky bits for texture, depending on your preference.

Return to the heat, add the white wine vinegar and stir in the crème fraîche and parsley until well mixed. Season with salt and pepper to taste and serve (with a bread roll if you like)!

The soup will keep in the fridge for up to 3 days.

TIP:

To keep your soup white, avoid using the darker green leaves from the leek.

SLOW COOKER CHICKEN BROTH

🕐 **15 MINS**　🍲 **4–8 HRS**　✕ **SERVES 4**

PER SERVING:
241 KCAL /29G CARBS

SPECIAL EQUIPMENT
3.5-litre slow cooker

300g skinless, boneless whole chicken breasts

1 onion, peeled and cut into 1cm (½in) dice

150g carrots, peeled and cut into 1cm (½in) dice

150g swede, peeled and cut into 1cm (½in) dice

2 celery sticks, trimmed and sliced

1 leek, trimmed and sliced

100g pearl barley

1 litre chicken stock (2 chicken stock cubes dissolved in 1 litre boiling water)

2 dried bay leaves

handful of fresh parsley, chopped

sea salt and freshly ground black pepper (*optional*)

Whether you're under the weather or not, this delicious broth is slimming-friendly comfort food at its best! We've started with a classic vegetable soup base of celery, carrots, leek and onion to rustle up this really easy, nutritious broth. Don't worry if you're short on time – you can always skip the veg prep by using a readymade soup pack instead. As long as your chicken bubbles away low and slow for 6–8 hours (or 4 hours on high!) until piping hot, tender and low-effort to shred, you'll be left with the same wholesome results.

Everyday Light

Put all the ingredients, except the parsley, salt and pepper, in the slow cooker pot, keeping the chicken breasts whole. Cover with the lid and cook for 4 hours on high, or 6–8 hours on low.

At the end of cooking time, remove the chicken breasts from the pot and place on a plate. Using 2 forks, pull the chicken apart into shreds. Return to the pot and stir in the parsley.

Taste and season with salt and pepper if required. Remove the bay leaves and serve.

IF YOU DON'T HAVE A SLOW COOKER
Alternatively, cook this in a heavy saucepan with a tight-fitting lid. Sauté the vegetables first in a little spray oil, then add all the other ingredients and bring to the boil then reduce the heat and simmer for 40–50 minutes with the lid on, until the chicken is cooked through and the vegetables and barley are tender and softened.

TIP:
Add a little hot water to the soup if you prefer a runnier consistency, adjusting the seasoning if necessary.

SOUPS

FREEZE ME

BATCH COOK

LOW CARB

DAIRY FREE

GLUTEN FREE

USE GF STOCK CUBE AND CHORIZO

SMOKY CHICKEN *and* CHORIZO SOUP

🕐 **10 MINS**   🍲 **45 MINS**   ✕ **SERVES 6**

PER SERVING:
155 KCAL / 14G CARBS

SPECIAL EQUIPMENT
Stick blender or food processor

low-calorie cooking spray
1 medium onion, peeled and chopped
2 garlic cloves, peeled and crushed
1 tbsp sweet smoked paprika
½ tsp mild chilli powder
3 skinless, boneless chicken thighs (visible fat removed), about 75g each
50g diced chorizo
1 litre chicken stock (1 chicken stock cube dissolved in 1 litre boiling water)
1 x 480g jar roasted red peppers in brine, drained and roughly chopped
200g potato, peeled and cut into small chunks
30g curly kale, shredded
sea salt and freshly ground black pepper

TO ACCOMPANY *(optional)*
60g wholemeal bread roll
(+ 146 kcal per roll)

TIPS:
You can find ready-diced chorizo in most supermarkets for convenience.

Add more chilli powder if you prefer things spicier.

Big on smoky flavour and low in calories, this comforting chicken soup is delicious come rain or shine. All that lovely smokiness comes from the winning combination of chorizo, paprika and roasted red peppers. Using jarred peppers keeps this recipe nice and effortless, and saves you from adding a baking tray to the washing-up pile! Once everything is cooked, all that's left to do is blend it until smooth, shred the chicken, add in the curly kale and serve.

Everyday Light ───────────────────

Spray a large saucepan with low-calorie cooking spray and place over a medium heat. Add the onion and cook for 8–10 minutes, until soft and golden, then add the garlic and cook for a further 2 minutes. Lower the heat, add the paprika and chilli powder and cook gently for a minute, stirring.

Increase the heat, add the chicken thighs and chorizo and cook for 3–4 minutes, until sealed and lightly browned on all sides. Add the stock, roasted red peppers and potato. Bring to the boil, then lower the heat, cover and simmer for 25 minutes or until the potato is soft and the chicken thighs are cooked.

Remove from the heat and remove the chicken thighs from the saucepan and set aside. Use a stick blender to blitz the soup until smooth in the saucepan. Alternatively, use a food processor to blitz the soup until smooth, then return it to the saucepan. (You may need to do this in batches depending on the size of your food processor.)

Shred the cooked chicken thighs using two forks and add back to the soup in the saucepan. Add the shredded kale and simmer for 3–4 minutes or until the kale is tender and the soup is piping hot. Season with salt and pepper, to taste.

Serve alone or with a wholemeal roll or other accompaniment of choice.

The soup will keep in the fridge for up to 3 days.

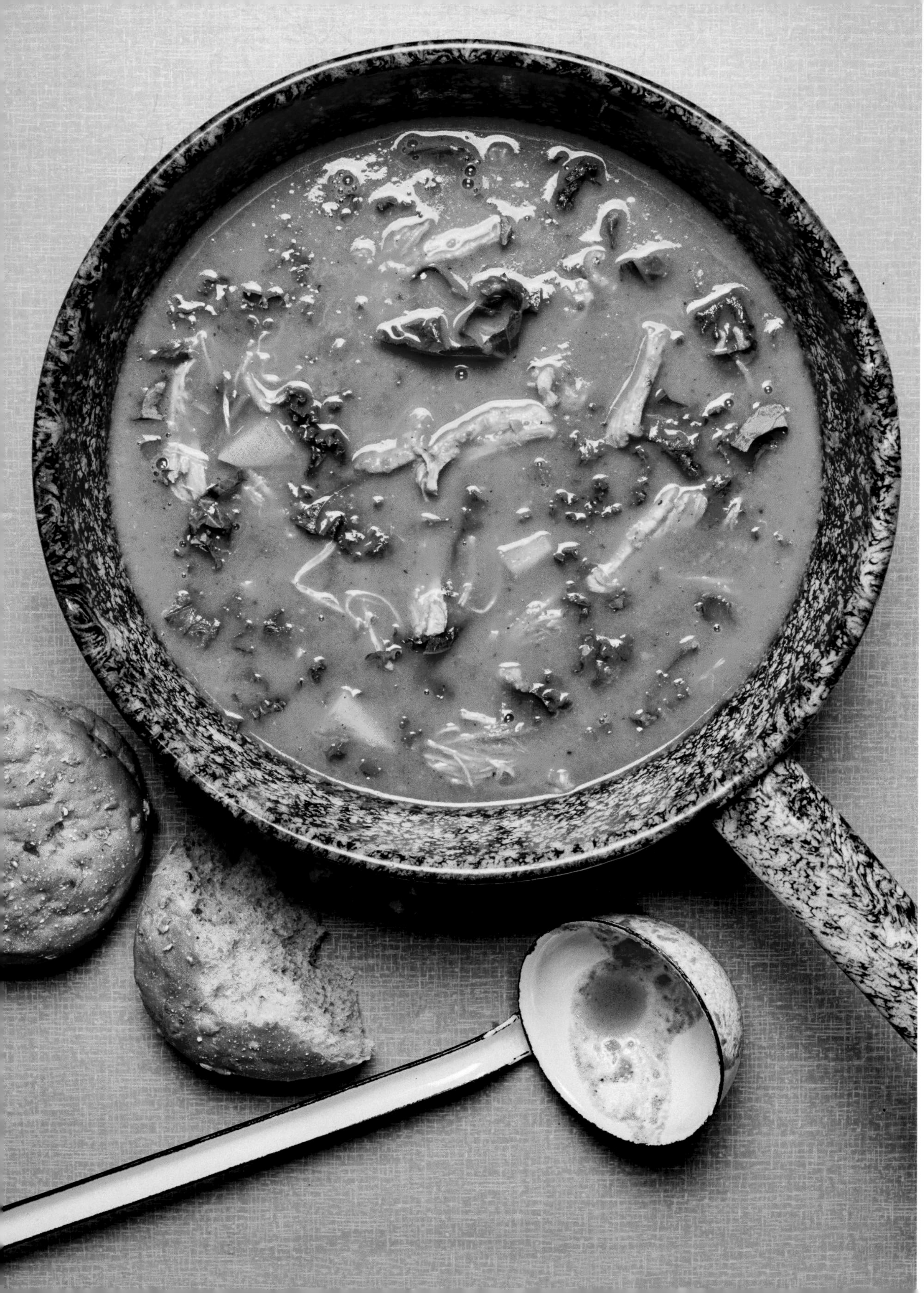

SWEET POTATO *and* MISO SOUP

🕐 **10 MINS**   🍲 **35 MINS**   ✕ **SERVES 4**

VEGGIE

VEGAN

FREEZE ME

BATCH COOK

DAIRY FREE

GLUTEN FREE

USE GF STOCK CUBE

PER SERVING:
176 KCAL /33G CARBS

SPECIAL EQUIPMENT
Stick blender or food processor

low-calorie cooking spray
1 large onion, peeled and roughly chopped
3 garlic cloves, peeled and crushed
2cm (¾in) piece of root ginger, peeled and finely chopped
small pinch of mild chilli powder
500g sweet potatoes, peeled and cut into 2cm (¾in) chunks
1 litre vegetable stock (1 low-salt vegetable stock cube dissolved in 1 litre boiling water)
4 tbsp white miso paste
freshly ground black pepper
1 spring onion, trimmed and finely chopped, to garnish (*optional*)

TO ACCOMPANY (*optional*)
60g wholemeal bread roll (+ 146 kcal per roll)

A little bit salty and a little bit sweet, this warming soup will keep your taste buds guessing with every slurp! White miso paste, made from fermented soya beans, is a common ingredient in Japanese-style cooking. It has a deep, savoury, umami flavour that balances beautifully with the sweet potatoes in this recipe. Blend it until it's silky smooth and velvety, then serve it with a crusty wholemeal roll on the side to wipe the bowl clean.

Everyday Light

Spray a large saucepan with low-calorie cooking spray and place over a medium heat. Add the onion and cook for 10 minutes, until soft and translucent, then add the garlic, ginger and chilli powder and cook for a further 1–2 minutes.

Add the sweet potato, stock and miso paste and stir until dissolved.

Bring to the boil, then lower the heat, cover and simmer for 20–25 minutes, until the sweet potato is soft.

Remove from the heat and use a stick blender to blitz the soup until smooth in the saucepan. Alternatively, use a food processor to blitz the soup until smooth, then return it to the saucepan. (You may need to do this in batches depending on the size of your food processor.) Season to taste with pepper (no need to season with salt as the miso paste adds saltiness), garnish with a little chopped spring onion (if using), and serve with a crusty wholemeal bread roll.

The soup will keep in the fridge for up to 3 days.

TIP:
A small pinch of mild chilli powder adds just a hint of warmth to this soup. You can add a little more if you'd prefer it hotter!

VEGGIE

VEGAN

FREEZE ME

BATCH COOK

DAIRY FREE

USE VEGAN SPREADABLE CHEESE

GLUTEN FREE

USE GF STOCK CUBE

VEGETABLE CHOWDER

🕐 **20 MINS**   🥘 **50 MINS**   ✕ **SERVES 6**

PER SERVING:
219 KCAL /26G CARBS

low-calorie cooking spray
1 medium onion, peeled and finely chopped
1 medium leek, trimmed, washed and finely chopped
1 medium carrot, peeled and finely diced
1 celery stick, trimmed and finely diced
2 garlic cloves, peeled and crushed
400g floury potatoes, peeled and cut into 1cm (½in) dice
700ml vegetable stock (2 vegetable stock cubes dissolved in 700ml boiling water)
1 dried bay leaf
1 tsp dried thyme
300ml skimmed milk
1 medium cauliflower, cut into bite-sized florets, stalks finely chopped and leaves shredded
1 x 198g tin sweetcorn, drained
125g reduced-fat mature Cheddar spreadable cheese
sea salt and freshly ground black pepper
pinch of cayenne pepper

TO ACCOMPANY *(optional)*
60g wholemeal bread roll (+ 146 kcal per roll)

You might expect to find cream in a chowder, but you won't find a drop in our slimming-friendly version! Don't worry though – we've made sure you're not missing out on any of the indulgent creaminess you want from a dish like this. Instead, we melt spreadable mature Cheddar cheese into our potato and cauliflower-based soup. The potatoes break down as they cook, thickening the soup without any need to blend. A pinch of cayenne pepper adds just the right hint of warmth.

Everyday Light

Spray a large saucepan with low-calorie cooking spray and place over a medium heat. Add the onion, leek, carrot, celery and garlic, stir and cook for 10–15 minutes, until softened and golden. Add the diced potato, vegetable stock, bay leaf, thyme and stir, then cover, bring to the boil, lower the heat and simmer for 20 minutes until the potato is tender.

Add the milk, cauliflower florets, stalks and leaves, and the sweetcorn. Stir well, cover and simmer for 10–15 minutes, stirring occasionally until the cauliflower is tender, and the leaves still retain their bright green colour.

Most of the potatoes will break up to thicken the chowder. Remove from the heat, stir in the spreadable cheese until completely melted and remove the bay leaf. Season well with salt and pepper, to taste, and sprinkle a pinch of cayenne pepper over the top. Serve, with bread rolls (if using).

The soup will keep in the fridge for up to 3 days.

TIP:
Use floury potatoes such as King Edward or Maris Piper; these will break up well to thicken the soup.

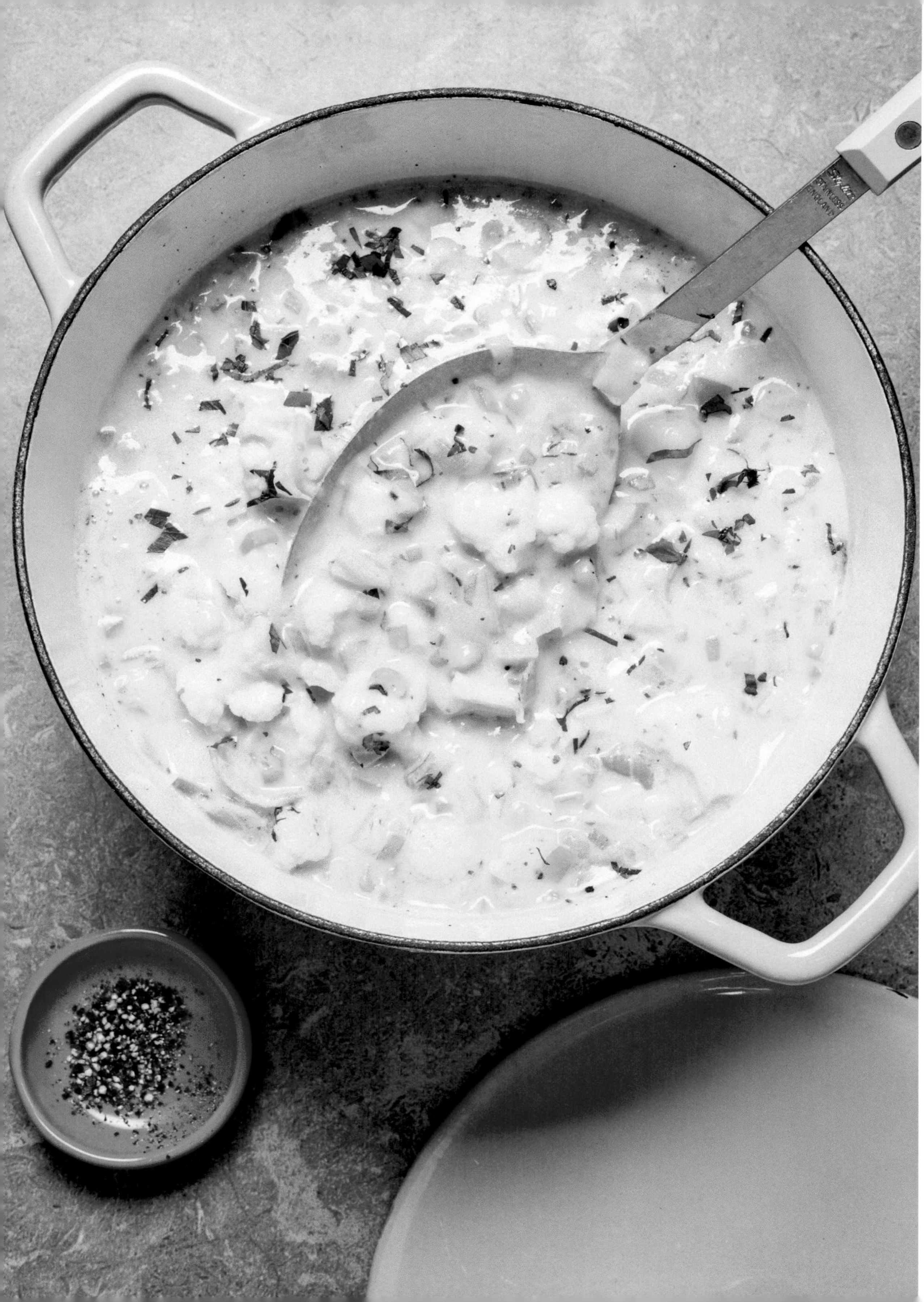

FREEZE
ME

BATCH
COOK

GLUTEN
FREE

USE GF
STOCK CUBE
AND FLOUR

SLOW COOKER CHEESEBURGER SOUP

🕐 **20 MINS**   🍲 **6 HRS**   ✕ **SERVES 6**

PER SERVING:
208 KCAL /24G CARBS

SPECIAL EQUIPMENT
3.5-litre slow cooker

low-calorie cooking spray
250g 5%-fat minced beef
3 potatoes (about 500g),
  peeled and diced
1 medium onion, peeled and
  diced
1 medium carrot, peeled and
  diced
1 celery stick, diced
3 garlic cloves, peeled and
  crushed
1 beef stock cube
3 tbsp tomato puree
600ml boiling water
1 tsp dried parsley
1 tsp dried basil
1 tsp smoked paprika
1 tsp ground cumin
1 tsp garlic powder
1 tbsp plain flour
150ml skimmed milk
50g reduced-fat Cheddar,
  grated
85g sliced gherkins
sea salt and freshly ground
  black pepper

If you're someone who loves a chunky soup just as much as a burger night, this recipe is bound to be up your street. We've used classic cheeseburger ingredients, including reduced-fat beef mince and lower-fat cheese, to put together a bowlful of utterly delicious, restaurant-inspired flavours. It's far lower in calories than a stacked burger, and surprisingly simple to make! Not everyone likes a gherkin, but they're definitely the perfect topping for this one-pot comfort food (try not to pick them off!).

Everyday Light

Spray a frying pan with low-calorie cooking spray and place over a medium heat. Add the mince and fry for 3–4 minutes until browned all over, breaking up the mince with a wooden spoon.

Add the browned beef, potatoes, onion, carrot, celery and garlic to the slow cooker, add the stock cube and tomato puree to the boiling water and stir until dissolved. Pour into the slow cooker. Add the parsley, basil, paprika, cumin, garlic powder and stir. Cover with the lid and cook on high for 5½ hours.

In a small jug, combine the flour and milk and stir, until combined. Add the grated cheese. Pour into the slow cooker and stir. Re-cover with the lid and cook for a further 30 minutes.

Season with salt and pepper, pour into bowls and top with the sliced gherkins.

TIP:
Add a little hot water to the soup if you prefer a runnier consistency, adjusting the seasoning if necessary.

SOUPS

46

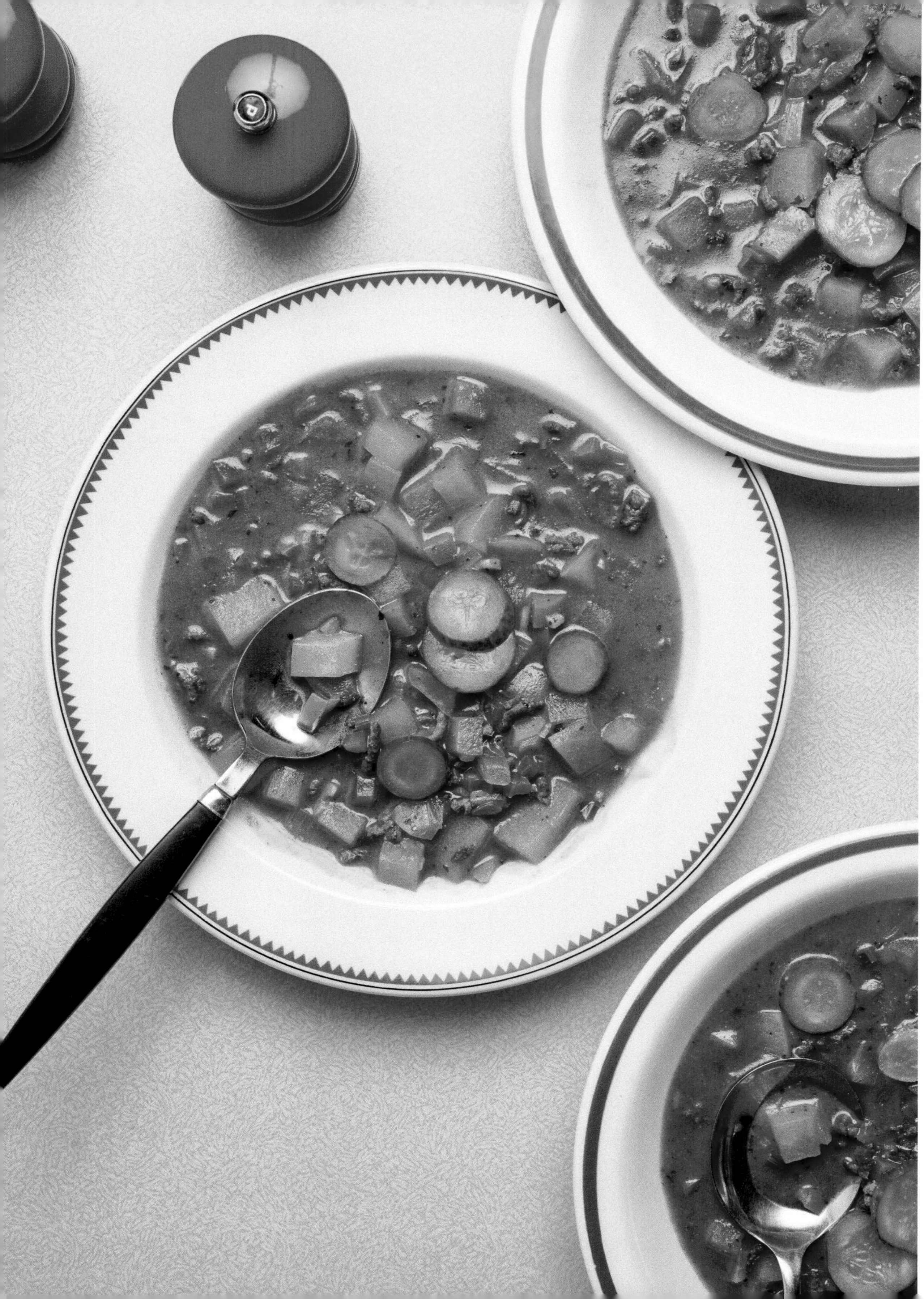

SLOW COOKED CHINESE-STYLE CHICKEN NOODLE SOUP

🕐 **10 MINS**   🍲 **1 HR**   ✕ **SERVES 4**

PER SERVING:
328 KCAL /39G CARBS

2 skinless chicken breasts (visible fat removed), about 175g each
1 small leek, trimmed and thinly sliced
250g carrots, peeled and cut into 1cm (½in) dice
150g frozen sweetcorn
200g mushrooms, thinly sliced
4 garlic cloves, peeled and crushed
4cm (1½in) piece of root ginger, peeled and finely grated
1 red or green chilli, deseeded and finely chopped
1 litre chicken stock (1 chicken stock cube dissolved in 1 litre boiling water)
3 tbsp oyster sauce
2 tbsp soy sauce
2 tbsp rice vinegar
1 x 300g pack of straight-to-wok noodles
handful of fresh coriander leaves, chopped, to serve

You can't beat the cosiness of noodle soup, especially when it's delightfully simple to make. Throw your ingredients into the pan, let them bubble away, and you'll have a slurp-worthy broth ready in a jiffy. The trick is to use veggies that'll hold their satisfying bite without turning mushy; we've gone for leek, diced carrots, mushrooms and sweetcorn. Warmed up with punchy garlic, ginger and chilli, the twirl-around-the-fork noodles make for an ultra-satisfying, fragrant bowlful.

Everyday Light

Place the chicken, vegetables, garlic, ginger and chilli in a large saucepan, pour in the hot stock and stir. Place over a medium heat and slowly bring to a simmer, then cover and reduce the heat to low. Cook for 45–50 minutes until the carrots are soft and the chicken is cooked through.

Remove the chicken from the pan, place on a plate, shred with two forks and return to the pan.

Stir in the oyster sauce, soy sauce, rice vinegar and noodles and simmer gently over a low heat for a minute or two to warm the noodles.

Divide among bowls, sprinkle over the coriander and serve.

TIPS:

This soup is intended to be a clear broth, but if you prefer a thicker soup you can thicken it with 1 tablespoon of cornflour mixed to a slurry with 1 tablespoon of water. Add this after removing the chicken breasts. You will need to simmer the soup in the saucepan for an extra few minutes, for the cornflour to cook.

If you've frozen the soup, after defrosting it, reheat loosely covered, in the microwave for 3–4 minutes, stirring, and adding the noodles halfway through, until piping hot.

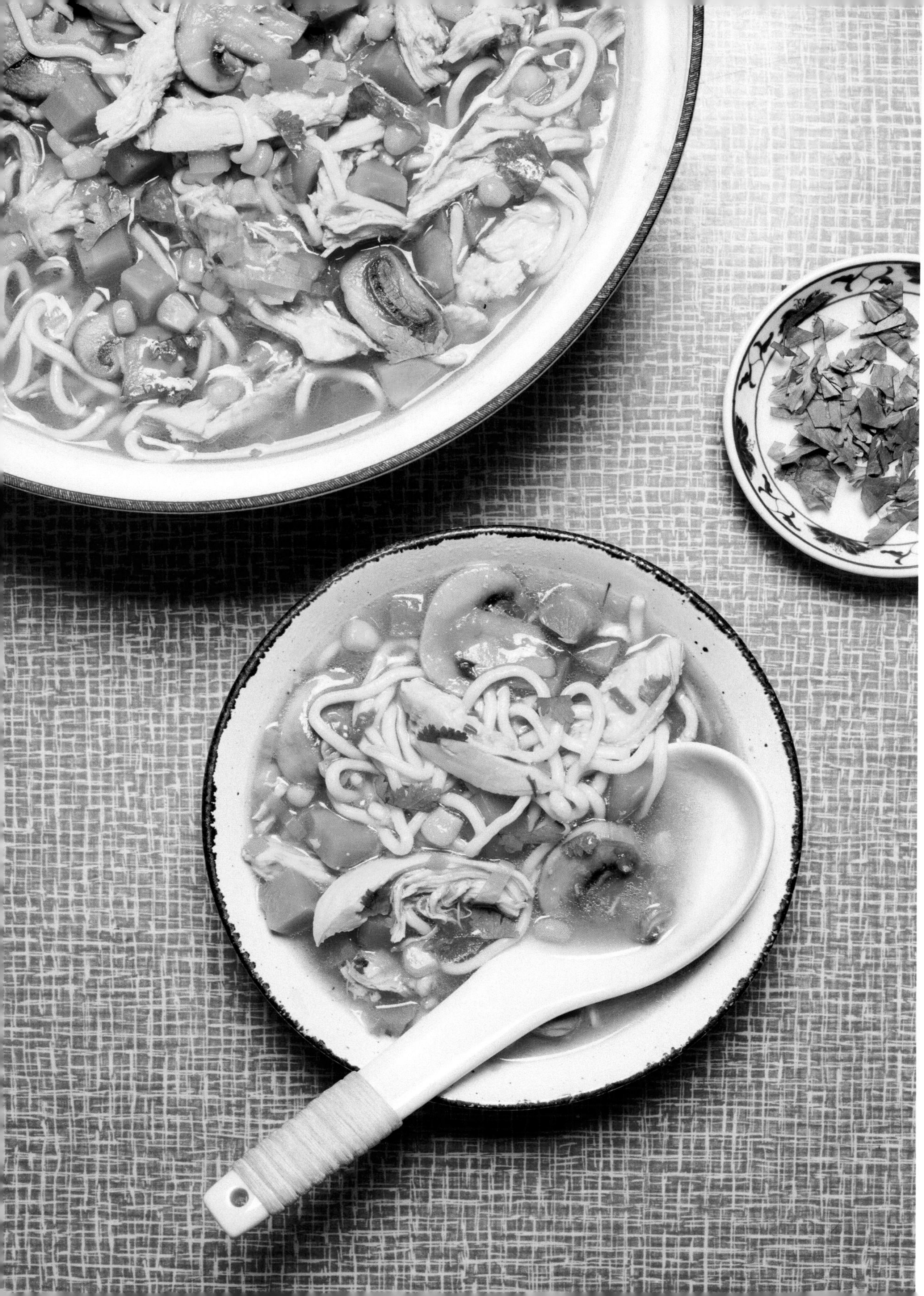

SLOW COOKER SMOKY FISH SOUP

🕐 **10 MINS**   🍲 **4–6 HRS**   ✕ **SERVES 4**

PER SERVING:
247 KCAL /22G CARBS

SPECIAL EQUIPMENT
3.5-litre slow cooker

1 onion, peeled and diced
2 carrots, peeled and sliced
4 garlic cloves, peeled and crushed
1 tbsp smoked sweet paprika
1 x 400g tin chopped tomatoes
2 tbsp tomato puree
1 x 400g tin chickpeas in water, drained and rinsed
300ml fish or vegetable stock (1 fish or vegetable stock cube dissolved in 300ml boiling water)
juice of 1 lemon
2 good handfuls of sliced curly kale
340g pack fish pie mix (or fish of choice)
freshly ground black pepper

TO ACCOMPANY
60g wholemeal bread roll (+ 146 kcal per roll)

You'll love every spoonful of this hearty and comforting Smoky Fish Soup. We like to save on time and effort by stirring in a shop-bought fish pie mix, but there's nothing to stop you using any fish you want. Just don't forget one key thing: make sure to use at least one smoked fish! That's what puts 'smoky' in the name. The vibrant sauce is spiced with paprika and garlic, to make every slurp rich with Spanish-inspired flavours. With carrots, onions, chickpeas and kale, there's no shortage of nutritious goodness here!

Weekly Indulgence

Put the onion, carrots, garlic, paprika, tomatoes, tomato puree, chickpeas and stock in the slow cooker pot, stir, cover with the lid and cook on high for 3–3½ hours or low for 5½–6 hours.

Add the lemon juice and stir in the sliced kale. Season with black pepper then add the fish. Stir and cover, then cook for a further 20–30 minutes until the fish is cooked through and the kale is tender.

Serve with a crusty bread roll.

IF YOU DON'T HAVE A SLOW COOKER
Alternatively, cook this in a saucepan on the hob. Cook for 40 minutes over a medium heat, adding the kale, lemon juice, black pepper and fish for the final 10 minutes.

SOUPS

50

STEWS

and

CASSEROLES

FREEZE
ME

BATCH
COOK

DAIRY
FREE

GLUTEN
FREE

USE GF
STOCK CUBE

HARISSA BEEF STEW

🕐 **20 MINS**   🍲 **VARIABLE**   ✕ **SERVES 6**

PER SERVING:
284 KCAL /22G CARBS

low-calorie cooking spray
1 medium onion, peeled and diced
4 garlic cloves, peeled and crushed
200g peeled and deseeded butternut squash, cut into 2cm (¾in) cubes
1 medium red pepper, deseeded and cut into 1cm (½in) dice
1 medium carrot, peeled and cut into 1cm (½in) dice
600g diced, lean braising or stewing steak, all visible fat removed
3 tbsp harissa paste (we used one with a medium heat)
600ml beef stock (200ml for pressure cooker method) (1 beef stock cube dissolved in 600/200ml boiling water)
1 x 400g tin chopped tomatoes
1 x 400g tin chickpeas in water, drained and rinsed
1 x 411g tin apricot halves in natural juice, drained and finely chopped
1 tbsp lemon juice
handful of fresh coriander leaves, roughly chopped
freshly ground black pepper

When you want big flavours for minimal effort, grab a jar of harissa paste! The warming blend of chillies, garlic and spices works its magic in this recipe, adding a subtle smokiness without ramping up the calories. Every bite of our comforting, slimming-friendly stew turns out to be deliciously tangy and a little sweet, with zinginess from the lemon juice and a gentle heat from the harissa. Don't forget you can use a spicier harissa paste if you like your food a little more fiery.

Everyday Light ──────────────

OVEN METHOD
🍲 **2 HOURS 25 MINS–2 HOURS 40 MINS**

SPECIAL EQUIPMENT
Large, deep casserole dish with tight-fitting lid (about 28cm/11in), suitable for hob and oven

Preheat the oven to 180°C (fan 160°C/gas mark 4).

Spray the large casserole dish with low-calorie cooking spray and place over a medium heat. Add the onion and garlic and cook for 10 minutes, stirring occasionally, until soft and golden, then add the butternut squash, red pepper and carrot and cook for 10 minutes until soft and the butternut squash is browning a little around the edges.

Add the beef and cook for 4–5 minutes until browned on all sides. Stir in the harissa paste, stock, tomatoes, chickpeas and apricots.

Cover with a tight-fitting lid and cook in the oven for 2–2¼ hours, or until the beef is tender, the vegetables are soft, and the sauce has thickened. Check occasionally to stir and make sure the stew isn't drying out. Add a little water if needed.

Remove from the oven and stir in the lemon juice and coriander leaves. Season to taste with pepper and serve.

The stew will keep in the fridge for up to 3 days.

PRESSURE-COOKER METHOD
🍲 55 MINS

SPECIAL EQUIPMENT
Pressure cooker

Spray the pressure cooker inner pot with low-calorie cooking spray.

Set to 'sauté', add the onion and garlic and cook for 5–10 minutes, stirring occasionally, until soft and golden, then add the butternut squash, red pepper and carrot and cook for 5–10 minutes until soft and the butternut squash is browning a little around the edges.

Add the beef and cook for 4–5 minutes, until browned on all sides. Stir in the harissa paste, stock, tomatoes, chickpeas and apricots.

Cover with the lid, lock and seal, and cook on high pressure for 30 minutes. Release the pressure and remove the lid. The beef should be tender, the vegetables soft, and the gravy thickened. If the stew is still a little runny, set to 'sauté' and continue to cook for a few more minutes until reduced and thickened.

Turn off the pressure cooker and stir in the lemon juice and coriander leaves. Season to taste with pepper and serve.

The stew will keep in the fridge for up to 3 days.

VEGGIE

USE
HENDERSON'S
RELISH AND
VEGETARIAN
ITALIAN HARD
CHEESE

FREEZE
ME

BATCH
COOK

DAIRY
FREE

USE DF
ITALIAN
HARD CHEESE

LENTIL STEW *with* HERBY DUMPLINGS

🕐 **30 MINS**   🍲 **2 HRS 25 MINS**   ✕ **SERVES 4**

PER SERVING:
465 KCAL /68G CARBS

SPECIAL EQUIPMENT
Casserole dish with tight-fitting lid (about 26cm/10in), suitable for hob and oven

low-calorie cooking spray
1 medium onion, peeled and finely chopped
3 garlic cloves, peeled and crushed
2 celery sticks, trimmed and finely diced
1 medium red pepper, deseeded and finely diced
1 medium green pepper, deseeded and finely diced
400g white mushrooms, finely chopped
2 medium carrots, peeled and cut into 2cm (¾in) chunks
2 small sweet potatoes (about 135g each), peeled and cut into 2cm (¾in) chunks
2 x 390g tins green lentils in water, drained and rinsed
1 x 400g tin chopped tomatoes
2 tbsp tomato puree
2 red wine stock pots
2 tbsp Worcestershire sauce or Henderson's relish
2 tsp balsamic vinegar
2 tsp mustard powder
400ml vegetable stock (150ml for slow cooker method) (1 veg stock cube dissolved in 400/150ml boiling water)
2 fresh thyme sprigs
1 fresh rosemary sprig
sea salt and freshly ground black pepper

We've packed so many vegetables, sweet potatoes and green lentils into this comforting stew, you'll never even notice it's completely meat free! While it simmers in the oven, it'll fill your kitchen with the most mouth-watering smell. Forget about using suet to make dumplings – our herby ones skip this ingredient and turn out beautifully light, fluffy and delicious. There's simply nothing better for dinner on a chilly, grey day!

Weekly Indulgence

Preheat the oven to 180°C (fan 160°C/gas mark 4).

Spray the casserole dish with low-calorie cooking spray and place over a medium heat. Add the onion, garlic, celery and peppers and cook for 10 minutes, until starting to soften.

Add the mushrooms and cook for 4–5 minutes, until softened and their juices have been released. Add the carrot, sweet potato, lentils, tomatoes, tomato puree, stock pots, Worcestershire sauce or Henderson's relish, balsamic vinegar, mustard powder, stock, thyme and rosemary sprigs. Season with salt and pepper and stir until the stock pots have dissolved.

Cover with a tight-fitting lid and place in the oven for about 2 hours, until the sweet potato is soft and tender, stirring occasionally.

While the stew is cooking, make the dumplings. Sift the flour and baking powder into a small bowl. Season with a little salt and pepper, then add the egg yolks and mix slightly with a fork. Using your fingertips, rub in the egg yolk until the mixture resembles breadcrumbs. Stir in the Parmesan, mustard powder, garlic granules, thyme and parsley.

Add 3–4 tablespoons of cold water, a little at a time, and stir with a round-bladed knife until it comes together to form a dough. You want a firm dough that's not too wet, so the amount of water you need will depend on the size of your egg yolks. Shape the dough into 4 equal-sized dumplings and set aside in the fridge for later.

List continues overleaf...

FOR THE HERBY DUMPLINGS

100g self-raising flour
¼ tsp baking powder
2 medium egg yolks
30g Parmesan, finely grated
½ tsp mustard powder
½ tsp garlic granules
1 tsp chopped fresh thyme leaves
1 tbsp chopped curly parsley

After the stew has been cooking for about 2 hours, remove the thyme and rosemary stalks and discard. Place the dumplings on top of the stew. Replace the lid and return to the oven for another 20–25 minutes, until the dumplings are cooked through and have puffed up. Remove the lid for the last 10 minutes if you want the dumplings to be golden. Serve. The stew will keep in the fridge for up to 2 days.

SLOW-COOKER METHOD
🍲 6-7 HOURS ON MEDIUM OR 5-6 HOURS ON HIGH

SPECIAL EQUIPMENT
3.5-litre slow cooker

Spray a large frying pan with low-calorie cooking spray and place over a medium heat. Add the onion, garlic, celery and peppers and cook for 10 minutes, until starting to soften.

Add the mushrooms and cook for 4-5 minutes, until softened and their juices have been released. Transfer the vegetables and any juices to the slow cooker.

Add the carrot, sweet potato, lentils, tomatoes, tomato puree, stock pots, Worcestershire sauce or Henderson's relish, balsamic vinegar, mustard powder, stock, thyme and rosemary sprigs. Season with salt and pepper and stir until the stock pots have dissolved.

Cover with the lid and cook on high for 3–3½ hours, until the sweet potato is soft and tender.

While the stew is cooking, make the dumplings. Sift the flour and baking powder into a small bowl. Season with a little salt and pepper, then add the egg yolks and mix slightly with a fork. Using your fingertips, rub in the egg yolk until the mixture resembles breadcrumbs. Stir in the Parmesan, mustard powder, garlic granules, thyme, and parsley.

Add 3–4 tbsp of cold water, a little at a time, and stir with a round-bladed knife, until it comes together to form a dough. You want a firm dough that's not too wet, so the amount of water you need will depend on the size of your egg yolks. Shape the dough into four equal-sized dumplings and set aside in the fridge for later.

After the stew has been cooking for 3–3½ hours, remove the thyme and rosemary stalks and discard. Place the dumplings on top of the stew. Replace the lid and continue to cook for a further 40 minutes, until the dumplings are cooked through and have puffed up. Serve.

TIPS:

Use a food processor to finely chop the mushrooms; it will save a lot of time!

If you've frozen the stew and dumplings, when reheating after defrosting, you may need to add a splash of water if it has dried out a little in the freezer.

STEWS *and* CASSEROLES

SPICY COD ONE-POT

🕐 **15 MINS**   🍲 **35 MINS**   ✕ **SERVES 4**

PER SERVING:
354 KCAL /33G CARBS

SPECIAL EQUIPMENT
Large, shallow casserole dish suitable for hob or large, deep frying pan, with tight-fitting lid (about 28cm/11in)

low-calorie cooking spray
1 medium onion, peeled and finely chopped
4 garlic cloves, peeled and crushed
1 red chilli, deseeded and finely chopped
1 x 480g jar roasted red peppers in brine, drained and finely diced
500g passata
2 x 400g tins butter beans in water, drained and rinsed
1 tsp Worcestershire sauce or Henderson's relish
1 tbsp sweet smoked paprika
1 tsp dried basil
1 tsp dried oregano
1 red wine stock pot
200g cherry tomatoes, halved
4 x skinless, boneless chunky cod loins (about 145g each)
80g baby spinach leaves
sea salt and freshly ground black pepper

TO ACCOMPANY
60g wholemeal bread roll
(+ 146 kcal per roll)

TIP:

This freezes well. When reheating after defrosting, you may need to add a splash of water if it has dried out a little in the freezer.

Once you've tried this all-in-one fish dinner, you'll want to add it to your meal plan every week. To get the best from the chunky cod loins, lay them gently on top of our paprika-infused roasted red pepper and bean sauce, and avoid stirring while it's all bubbling away. That way, when you plate it up, it'll arrive in one piece – to enjoy by itself, or with garlic green beans or a wholemeal roll.

Everyday Light ───────────────

Spray the casserole dish or frying pan with low-calorie cooking spray and place over a medium heat. Add the onion and fry for 10 minutes until softening and golden, then add the garlic and red chilli and cook for a further 1–2 minutes. Add the roasted red peppers, passata, butter beans, Worcestershire sauce or Henderson's relish, paprika, basil, oregano and the stock pot (no need to dissolve it in water). Season with salt and pepper and stir until the stock pot has dissolved, then cover with a tight-fitting lid, lower the heat and simmer gently for 10 minutes until thickened.

Stir in the cherry tomatoes and place the cod loins on top, nestling them into the sauce. Cover with the tight-fitting lid and simmer gently for 10–12 minutes, until the cod is cooked. Don't stir, otherwise the cod loins will break up. Timings may vary a little depending on the thickness of your cod loins but take care not to overcook them as fish cooks quickly. The cod should be white and opaque, and flake when a knife is inserted.

Place the spinach leaves around the cod loins, pushing the spinach into the sauce. Take care not to break up the fish. Remove from the heat, cover and allow the spinach to wilt in the heat in the pan for a minute or two. Serve, using a fish slice to lift the cod loins as they are delicate.

The dish will keep in the fridge for up to 2 days.

VEGGIE

VEGAN

FREEZE ME

BATCH COOK

DAIRY FREE

GLUTEN FREE
USE GF STOCK CUBE

VEGGIE BLACK BEAN STEW

🕐 **20 MINS**   🍲 **40 MINS**   ✕ **SERVES 4**

PER SERVING:
385 KCAL / 50G CARBS

SPECIAL EQUIPMENT
28cm (11in) shallow casserole dish with tight-fitting lid

low-calorie cooking spray
1 onion, peeled and cut into large dice
2 peppers (mixed colours), deseeded and cut into large dice
2 green chillies, deseeded and finely chopped
4 garlic cloves, peeled and crushed
5cm (2in) piece of root ginger, peeled and grated
1 tsp dried thyme
1 tsp ground cumin
1 x 400g tin chopped tomatoes
1 x 400g tin light coconut milk
200ml vegetable stock (1 vegetable stock cube dissolved in 200ml boiling water)
400g sweet potatoes, peeled and cut into 2.5cm (1in) dice
125g baby corn, cut into 1.5cm (¾in) chunks
2 x 400g tins black beans in water, drained and rinsed
juice of 1 lime
handful of fresh coriander, roughly chopped
sea salt and freshly ground black pepper

You won't want to wait until winter to enjoy this flavoursome stew. A warming pot of creamy coconut flavours, you also get tangy lime, ginger, hints of chilli and soft sweet potato chunks in every serving. We've ramped up the protein with budget-friendly tinned black beans and added plenty of colourful veggies into the mix. Lighter in calories than you might think, our dish avoids heavier full-fat coconut milk, so it's silky and satisfying without taking you off track.

Everyday Light

Spray the casserole dish with low-calorie cooking spray and place over a medium heat. Add the onion and peppers and fry for 5 minutes until soft, then add the chilli, garlic, ginger, thyme and cumin and cook for another minute until fragrant. Add the tomatoes, coconut milk and stock, stir in the sweet potatoes and baby corn and bring to the boil.

Reduce the heat to a simmer, cover with a tight-fitting lid and cook for 20 minutes.

Stir in the black beans and lime juice. If the sauce looks too thin, leave uncovered. Otherwise, replace the lid and continue cooking for a further 10 minutes or until the sweet potatoes are cooked through, but not falling apart.

Taste and season with salt and pepper, if needed. Stir in the coriander and serve.

The stew will keep in the fridge for up to 3 days.

ITALIAN-STYLE SAUSAGE STEW

🕐 **15 MINS**   🍲 **1 HR 5 MINS**   ✕ **SERVES 4**

PER SERVING:
442 KCAL /59G CARBS

SPECIAL EQUIPMENT
28cm (11in) shallow casserole dish with tight-fitting lid, suitable for use on the hob

low-calorie cooking spray
8 reduced-fat pork sausages
2 medium onions, peeled and diced
2 peppers (any colour), deseeded and diced
2 carrots, peeled and sliced
1 courgette, sliced
4 garlic cloves, peeled and crushed
1 tsp dried oregano
1 tsp dried rosemary
1 x 400g tin chopped tomatoes
750ml chicken stock (2 chicken stock cubes dissolved in 750ml boiling water)
1 tbsp balsamic vinegar
150g dried pasta shapes (e.g., fusilli, penne or macaroni)
1 x 400g tin cannellini beans in water, drained and rinsed
sea salt and freshly ground black pepper
10g Parmesan, grated (*optional*)

Stews are a great way of sneaking extra veggies into fussy eaters, and this Italian-inspired recipe is no exception! We've used peppers, onions and courgettes, but you could throw in any leftover vegetables from the fridge drawer to make your version even more budget-friendly. Bulked out with beans and whatever kind of pasta that you have in the cupboard, you'll easily feed a family of 4 with just one pack of low-fat sausages.!

Weekly Indulgence

Spray the casserole dish with low-calorie cooking spray.

Over a medium to high heat, fry the sausages for around 4–5 minutes until nicely browned. They don't need to be fully cooked through as they will be returned to the pan later. Remove and set aside.

Give the pan another spray with low-calorie cooking spray, then add the onions, peppers, carrots and courgette and sauté for 6–8 minutes until the vegetables are starting to soften.

Add the garlic and herbs and continue to cook for 1 minute.

Add the tomatoes, stock and balsamic vinegar and bring to a simmer.

Cut the sausages into 3 and return to the pan. Cover and cook for 35 minutes.

Add the pasta and beans and stir well. Cover and cook for a further 15–20 minutes (this will depend on the type of pasta you use). Remember that the pasta will absorb some liquid, so add a little more water if you think it is looking too dry.

Taste and season with some salt and pepper if desired.

Serve sprinkled with some grated Parmesan, if you wish.

TIP:
This works well with potatoes instead of pasta. Simply cut into 2cm (¾in) chunks and add with the sausage pieces.

STEWS *and* **CASSEROLES**

HAM *and* BEAN CASSEROLE

🕐 **15 MINS***   🍲 **VARIABLE**   ✕ **SERVES 4**

***PLUS SOAKING BEANS OVERNIGHT**

FREEZE ME

BATCH COOK

DAIRY FREE

GLUTEN FREE

USE GF STOCK CUBE

PER SERVING:
685 KCAL /72G CARBS

400g dried mixed beans, soaked overnight

low-calorie cooking spray

1 large onion, peeled and finely chopped

2 celery sticks, trimmed and finely chopped

5 carrots, finely chop 3 of them, cut the other 2 into chunks

2–3 dried bay leaves

500ml ham or chicken stock (1 ham or chicken stock cube dissolved in 500ml boiling water)

750g gammon joint, all excess fat removed

2 tbsp white wine vinegar

A twist on our popular Campfire Stew recipe, this warming one-pot wonder is a regular midweek meal in our house. Dried mixed beans are an inexpensive ingredient that you can keep in the cupboard until you fancy a dinner full of protein and goodness. Leave them to soak in water overnight, so they're ready to add into the dish along with your gammon joint.

Special Occasion

SLOW-COOKER METHOD
🍲 **6–7 HOURS ON MEDIUM OR 5–6 HOURS ON HIGH**

SPECIAL EQUIPMENT
3.5-litre slow cooker, stick blender

Drain the soaked beans well and rinse them a couple of times in fresh water. Put the rinsed, soaked beans in a pan and cover with cold water. Bring to the boil and cook for 5–10 minutes, then drain.

If your slow cooker has a sauté function, spray with low-calorie cooking spray and sauté the onion, celery and the finely chopped carrots for 5–10 minutes until the onion is browned. if there is no sauté function, fry the onion, celery and carrots in a frying pan then transfer them to the slow cooker.

Put the bay leaves, boiled beans and all the remaining ingredients except the white wine vinegar and gammon joint in the slow cooker and mix well, then add the gammon joint and cook on medium for 6–7 hours or on high for 5–6 hours.

If the gammon is still in one piece, remove it and chop it up into chunks, or shred it with two forks, and return it to the slow cooker. Stir in the white wine vinegar and remove the bay leaves.

Remove 2–3 ladles of the beans into a bowl and blitz with a stick blender until smooth. Return to the slow cooker to instantly thicken. Enjoy!

The casserole will keep in the fridge for up to 3 days.

PRESSURE-COOKER METHOD
🍲 45 MINS

SPECIAL EQUIPMENT
Pressure cooker, stick blender

Drain the soaked beans well and rinse them a couple of times in fresh water.

Spray the pot with low-calorie cooking spray and sauté the onion, celery and 2 of the finely chopped carrots for about 10 minutes, until the onion is cooked.

Add the drained beans and stir for a minute or two, then add the gammon, placing it on top of the beans. Add the stock: it should just cover the beans. Cover and cook on manual for 30 minutes then natural pressure release.

Add the white wine vinegar and the remaining chopped carrot and cook for 5 minutes, then natural pressure release.

If the gammon is still in one piece, remove it and chop it up into chunks, or shred it with two forks, and return it to the pressure cooker. Discard the bay leaves.

Remove 2 or 3 ladles of the beans into a bowl and blitz with a stick blender until smooth. Return to the pot to instantly thicken. Enjoy!

The casserole will keep in the fridge for up to 3 days.

FREEZE
ME

STEW ONLY

BATCH
COOK

DAIRY
FREE

USE DF
YOGHURT

GLUTEN
FREE

PERSIAN-STYLE LAMB STEW

🕐 **15 MINS**   🍲 **VARIABLE**   ✕ **SERVES 4**

PER SERVING:
424 KCAL /40G CARBS

low-calorie cooking spray
2 medium onions, peeled and
   finely chopped
2 garlic cloves, peeled and
   crushed
1 red chilli, deseeded and
   finely chopped
1 tsp ground cumin
1 tsp ground cinnamon
1 tsp ground coriander
½ tsp ground turmeric
450g diced leg of lamb, all
   visible fat removed
1 x 400g tin chickpeas, drained
   and rinsed
1 x 411g tin apricot halves in
   natural juice, drained
1 x 400g tin chopped tomatoes
1 tbsp tomato puree
finely grated zest and juice of
   1 large orange
500ml chicken stock (400ml for
   slow cooker method)
   (1 chicken stock cube
   dissolved in 500/400ml
   boiling water)
100g dried giant couscous
sea salt and freshly ground
   black pepper

FOR THE TOP
80g fat-free natural yoghurt
10g fresh mint leaves, stalks
   removed
80g pomegranate seeds

Whether it's from the oven or simmered in the slow cooker, you can trust this hearty stew to leave everyone feeling full and satisfied. The lamb is cooked in a warming broth until fall-off-the-fork tender and seasoned with family-friendly herbs and spices. We've added sweet apricots, orange juice and zest, and a tantalising topping of pomegranate seeds for each bowlful, to cut through the savoury flavours. It's always a good idea to stash leftover batches in the freezer, they'll warm you right up!

Weekly Indulgence

OVEN METHOD
🍲 **2 HOURS–2 HOURS 30 MINS**

SPECIAL EQUIPMENT
Large casserole dish with a tight-fitting lid (about 28cm/11in), suitable for hob and oven

Preheat the oven to 180°C (fan 160°C/gas mark 4).

Spray the casserole dish with low-calorie cooking spray and place over a medium heat.

Add the onions and fry for 10 minutes, stirring occasionally, until slightly softened and golden brown, then add the garlic, chilli, cumin, cinnamon, coriander and turmeric, stir well and cook for 1–2 minutes. Add the lamb to the onion and spices and cook for 2–3 minutes to seal on all sides.

Add the chickpeas, apricots, chopped tomatoes, tomato puree, orange zest, orange juice and stock to the casserole dish. Season well with salt and pepper and stir to combine all the ingredients, put the lid on the casserole dish and place in the oven. Cook for 1 hour 30 minutes, then stir in the couscous. Cover and cook for another 30 minutes, then check the lamb is tender and the couscous is cooked. If not, return to the oven for another 10–15 minutes.

Place the stew on serving plates and top with a small spoonful of yoghurt, fresh mint leaves and pomegranate seeds. The stew will keep in the fridge for up to 3 days.

STEWS *and* CASSEROLES

SLOW-COOKER METHOD
🍲 **5–6 HOURS**

SPECIAL EQUIPMENT
3.5-litre slow cooker

If your slow cooker has a sauté function, spray with low-calorie cooking spray and cook the onion for 10 minutes, stirring occasionally, until slightly softened and golden brown. Add the garlic, chilli, cumin, cinnamon, coriander and turmeric, stir well and cook for 1–2 minutes, then add the lamb to the onion and spices and cook for 2–3 minutes to seal on all sides. If there is no sauté function, follow the first steps using a frying pan and transfer it to the slow cooker. Add the chickpeas, apricots, chopped tomatoes, tomato puree, orange zest, orange juice and stock to the slow cooker. Season well with salt and pepper and stir to combine all the ingredients. Cover with the lid and cook on high for 5–6 hours. An hour before the end of cooking, stir in the couscous and allow to cook for the remaining hour.

Place the stew on serving plates and top with a small spoonful of yoghurt, fresh mint leaves and pomegranate seeds.

The stew will keep in the fridge for up to 3 days.

TIPS:

You can buy pomegranate seeds in boxes from most supermarkets. They are convenient to use as it saves you having to remove them from a whole pomegranate, which can be a fiddly job.

If you've frozen the stew, once defrosted and reheated, add the yoghurt, pomegranate seeds and mint leaves.

BEEF *and* HORSERADISH STEW

 15 MINS    **VARIABLE**   ✕ **SERVES 4**

PER SERVING:
400 KCAL /36G CARBS

low-calorie cooking spray
500g diced beef, all visible fat removed
2 medium onions, peeled and chopped
4 garlic cloves, peeled and crushed
2 medium carrots, peeled and thickly sliced
300g parsnips, peeled and cut into 2cm (¾in) chunks
200g white mushrooms, quartered or halved depending on their size
300g new potatoes, quartered or halved depending on size
900ml beef stock (1 beef stock cube dissolved in 900ml boiling water)
1 beef stock pot
2 tbsp tomato puree
1 tbsp Dijon mustard
1 tbsp balsamic vinegar
1 tbsp Worcestershire sauce or Henderson's relish
2 tsp dried thyme
2 dried bay leaves
3 tbsp creamed horseradish sauce
sea salt and freshly ground black pepper

If you're flicking through this book to find hearty, wholesome soul food, you'll want to bookmark this page. A thick, rich stew of tender beef chunks and vibrant, earthy veggies, we've added punchy, creamed horseradish for a tangy twist. The smell of all those flavourful ingredients bubbling away into a comforting, homemade gravy is too good to miss! Bake everything together in a casserole dish, or pop it all into your pressure cooker for a midweek wintery-warmer in a fraction of the time.

Weekly Indulgence

OVEN METHOD
🍲 **2 HOURS 15 MINS–2 HOURS 45 MINS**

SPECIAL EQUIPMENT
Large casserole dish with a tight-fitting lid (about 28cm/11in), suitable for hob and oven

Preheat the oven to 180°C (fan 160°C/gas mark 4).

Spray the casserole dish with low-calorie cooking spray and place over a medium-high heat. When hot, add the beef and fry for 3–4 minutes, turning, to seal and brown on all sides. Lower the heat to medium and add the onions, scraping up any meaty bits from the bottom of the casserole dish and stirring in. Cook for about 5 minutes, until the onion softens and turns golden, then add the garlic, stir and cook for a further 1–2 minutes. Add the carrots, parsnips, mushrooms and potatoes, and cook for 4–5 minutes.

In a measuring jug, mix the hot stock, stock pot, tomato puree, Dijon mustard, balsamic vinegar, Worcestershire sauce or Henderson's relish, thyme and bay leaves. Stir until the stock pot has dissolved, then pour into the casserole dish and stir it into the beef and vegetables. Cover with a tight-fitting lid and place in the oven for 2–2½ hours. Check occasionally to make sure the stew isn't drying out, adding a little more water if needed. The stew will be ready when the beef and vegetables are tender, and the gravy has reduced and thickened.

Remove from the oven and stir in the creamed horseradish sauce until completely blended. Season to taste with salt and pepper if needed and remove the bay leaves. Serve.

The stew will keep in the fridge for up to 2 days.

PRESSURE-COOKER METHOD
🍲 45 MINS

SPECIAL EQUIPMENT
Pressure cooker

Spray the pressure cooker with low-calorie cooking spray.

Take the beef and sauté for 3–4 minutes, stirring, to seal and brown on all sides. Add the onions, scraping up any meaty bits from the bottom of the pot and stirring in, and sauté for about 5 minutes, until the onion softens and turns golden, then add the garlic, stir and sauté for a further 1–2 minutes.

Add the carrots, parsnips, mushrooms and potatoes and sauté for 4–5 minutes.

In a measuring jug, mix the hot stock, stock pot, tomato puree, Dijon mustard, balsamic vinegar, Worcestershire sauce or Henderson's relish, thyme and bay leaves. Stir until the stock pot has dissolved, then pour into the pressure cooker and stir into the beef and vegetables. Close the lid on the pressure cooker and lock. Turn the valve to 'sealing', set to pressure cook, high, and set the timer for 30 minutes.

After 30 minutes cooking, release the pressure using quick pressure release. The stew will be ready when the beef and vegetables are tender and the gravy has thickened. If the stew is still too runny, sauté for a few more minutes with the lid off, until reduced and thickened.

Stir in the creamed horseradish sauce until completely blended. Season to taste with salt and pepper if needed and remove the bay leaves. Serve.

The stew will keep in the fridge for up to 2 days.

TIPS:

Use new potatoes as they will retain their shape during cooking; other varieties such as King Edward or Maris Piper will break up.

If you've frozen the stew, when reheating after defrosting, you may need to add a splash of water if it has dried out a little in the freezer.

If you want to cook this recipe in a slow cooker, brown the beef and vegetables in a large frying pan first, then add them to the slow cooker with the remaining ingredients. Cover and cook for 4–5 hours on high or 6–7 hours on low, until the beef and vegetables are tender, and the gravy has thickened. Then stir in the horseradish sauce, season, remove the bay leaves and serve.

SLOW COOKER PEPPERED BEEF *with* PASTA

🕐 **10 MINS**   🍲 **3½–7 HRS**   ✕ **SERVES 4**

PER SERVING:
457 KCAL /50G CARBS

SPECIAL EQUIPMENT
3.5-litre slow cooker

low-calorie cooking spray
400g lean diced beef
1 onion, peeled and sliced
250g mushrooms, sliced
500ml beef stock (1 beef stock
  cube dissolved in 500ml
  boiling water)
2 tbsp cornflour, mixed to a
  slurry with 2 tbsp water
1 tsp freshly ground black
  pepper
200g half-fat crème fraîche
200g small pasta shapes, e.g.,
  penne or fusilli

There's just something about beef that's been slow cooked for hours! For this easy-peasy pasta dish, we've simmered lean diced beef in a creamy, peppery sauce until it's velvety soft and melts in your mouth. By using half-fat crème fraîche we've kept things slimming friendly, without losing out on the satisfying silkiness of the sauce. Feel free to raid your cupboard for small pasta shapes like penne or fusilli – any kind will do!

Weekly Indulgence

Spray a frying pan with low-calorie cooking spray and place over a high heat. Add the beef and quickly fry until browned on all sides.

Add to the slow cooker pot, along with the onion and mushrooms. Pour in the hot stock and cornflour slurry and stir well. Cover with the lid and cook on high for 3½–4 hours, or low for 6–7 hours, until the beef is tender.

Stir in the black pepper and crème fraîche. Add the pasta and re-cover with the lid. If you have been cooking on low, turn up to the high setting. Cook for a further 40 minutes, stirring halfway through. The pasta should be cooked, and the sauce should have thickened. Serve!

TIP:
We prefer to brown the beef before adding it to the slow cooker, as it improves the flavour and texture of the dish. If you are pushed for time, you can skip this step!

STEWS *and* CASSEROLES

VEGGIE

VEGAN

FREEZE ME

BATCH COOK

DAIRY FREE

GLUTEN FREE

USE GF STOCK CUBE/POT

BEAN *and* MUSHROOM BOURGUIGNON

🕐 **20 MINS**   🍲 **1 HR 10 MINS**   ✕ **SERVES 4**

PER SERVING:
240 KCAL / 36G CARBS

SPECIAL EQUIPMENT
28cm (11in) shallow casserole dish or sauté pan with a tight-fitting lid

low-calorie cooking spray
1 onion, peeled and finely diced
2 celery sticks, sliced
250g carrots, peeled and thickly sliced
4 garlic cloves, peeled and crushed
250g chestnut mushrooms, quartered
2 tbsp tomato puree
750ml vegetable stock (1 vegetable stock cube dissolved in 750ml boiling water)
1 red wine stock pot
1 tbsp fresh thyme leaves
12 small round shallots, peeled and left whole
2 dried bay leaves
2 x 400g tins cannellini beans in water, drained and rinsed
2 tsp red wine vinegar
2 tsp Henderson's relish
1 tbsp cornflour, mixed to a slurry with 1 tbsp water
sea salt and freshly ground black pepper

TO ACCOMPANY
60g wholemeal bread roll (+ 146 kcal per roll)

A vegan version of a French-inspired classic, this Bean and Mushroom Bourguignon is warming and hearty. To keep fuss and mess to a minimum, you'll only need one casserole dish to throw all the ingredients in. It's well worth taking your time to let the onions, celery and carrots cook down nice and slowly – trust us, it'll make your sauce darker, richer and more flavourful. You'll want a crusty bread roll to make the most of every last drop!

Everyday Light ──────────

Spray the casserole dish or sauté pan with low-calorie cooking spray and place over a medium-low heat. Add the onion, celery, carrots and a pinch of salt, and fry gently for about 15 minutes, until the onions are soft and well browned – but not burnt! Add the garlic and mushrooms and cook for 2 minutes, until the mushrooms begin to release their moisture, then stir in the tomato puree. Add the vegetable stock, red wine stock pot and thyme, stir in the whole shallots and bring to the boil. Reduce the heat to a simmer, pop in the bay leaves, cover with a tight-fitting lid and simmer for 40 minutes.

Add the beans, red wine vinegar and Henderson's relish. Bring back to a simmer and cook, uncovered, for 10 minutes. The carrots and shallots should be tender.

Stir in the cornflour slurry and allow to cook for another 2 minutes, until the sauce is thick and rich. Taste and season with salt and pepper, if required. Remove the bay leaves and serve with bread rolls, if you wish: we've suggested this accompaniment to ensure this is a true, all-in-one recipe. You can enjoy this dish with any accompaniment you like, but don't forget to adjust the calories accordingly.

The dish will keep in the fridge for up to 3 days.

TIPS:

You can use Worcestershire sauce instead of Henderson's sauce, but this is not gluten free or vegetarian.

Swap cannellini beans for butter beans, if you like, and you can swap the fresh thyme for 1 tsp of dried thyme.

VEGGIE

VEGAN

USE VEGAN
YOGHURT

**FREEZE
ME**

**BATCH
COOK**

**DAIRY
FREE**

USE DF
YOGHURT

**GLUTEN
FREE**

USE GF STOCK
CUBES

SLOW COOKER VEGETARIAN GOULASH

🕐 **15 MINS** 🍲 **4–6½ HRS** ✕ **SERVES 4**

PER SERVING:
321 KCAL /49G CARBS

SPECIAL EQUIPMENT
3.5-litre slow cooker

1 onion, peeled and diced
200g sweet potatoes, peeled and cut into 2.5cm (1in) dice
200g new potatoes, cut into 2.5cm (1in) dice
2 carrots, peeled and cut into 5mm (¼in)-thick slices
4 garlic cloves, peeled and crushed
1 tsp dried oregano
2 tbsp smoked sweet paprika
1 tbsp tomato puree
200ml vegetable stock (1 vegetable stock cube dissolved in 200ml boiling water)
2 x 400g tins chopped tomatoes
1 red pepper, deseeded and diced
2 x 400g tins butter beans in water, drained and rinsed

TO SERVE
4 tbsp fat-free Greek yoghurt
handful of fresh flat-leaf parsley, chopped

Traditionally, goulash is a hearty stew of beef and veggies, but our vegetarian version packs in extra goodness by swapping out the meat for tender sweet potatoes and creamy butter beans. We've let all the ingredients simmer away in the slow cooker, until the sauce is rich, tomatoey and bursting with the smoky flavour of paprika. Don't skip the swirl of Greek yoghurt right before serving – the fresh tanginess of the yoghurt is just what you need to balance the sweetness of the stew.

Everyday Light

Place all of the ingredients (except the red pepper, butter beans, Greek yoghurt and parsley) in the slow cooker pot. Stir, cover with the lid and cook on high for 3½ hours or low for 6 hours.

Add the red pepper and butter beans, replace the lid and cook for a further 30 minutes.

Served topped with Greek yoghurt and parsley.

SLOW COOKER VEGETARIAN WHITE CHILLI

🕐 **15 MINS**   🍲 **3½–6 HRS**   ✕ **SERVES 4**

USE VEGAN
CREAM CHEESE

USE DF CREAM
CHEESE

USE GF
STOCK POT

PER SERVING:
331 KCAL /35G CARBS

SPECIAL EQUIPMENT
3.5-litre slow cooker

1 medium red pepper, deseeded and diced
1 medium green pepper, deseeded and diced
1 medium onion, peeled and diced
1 medium carrot, peeled and diced
1 celery stick, diced
4 garlic cloves, peeled and crushed
1 x 400g tin cannellini beans in water, drained and rinsed (drained weight about 235g)
1 x 400g tin black beans, drained and rinsed (drained weight about 235g)
1 x 215g tin kidney beans, drained and rinsed (drained weight about 130g)
1 tbsp ground cumin
2 tsp smoked paprika
2 tsp mild chilli powder
2 tsp garlic granules
2 tsp dried oregano
1 tsp ground coriander
¼ tsp freshly ground black pepper
1 vegetable stock pot
1 tbsp tomato puree
250ml boiling water
juice of 1 lime
200g reduced-fat cream cheese
salt, to taste

TO ACCOMPANY *(optional)*
10g lightly salted tortilla chips (+ 48 kcal per serving)

Bookmark this page if you can't get enough of chilli con carne. This slimming-friendly Vegetarian White Chilli adds a creamy twist to the midweek staple, without compromising on Mexican-inspired flavours – and it's ready in four simple steps! Leave the vegetables, beans and spices to mingle for hours, before stirring in the magic ingredient: reduced-fat cream cheese. A squeeze of lime is the perfect finishing touch to give the silky sauce some zing. We've served tortilla chips on the side, but there's nothing to stop you using them as a spoon!

Everyday Light ────────────

Put all the vegetables and beans in the pot of your slow cooker. Sprinkle over the herbs and spices.

Add the stock pot and tomato puree to the boiling water and stir until dissolved. Pour over the vegetables and beans. Stir, cover with the lid and cook for 3½ hours on high or for 6 hours on low.

The vegetables should be soft. Add the lime juice and cream cheese and stir to combine. Season with salt to taste and serve.

IF YOU DON'T HAVE A SLOW COOKER
Alternatively, cook this in a large frying pan. Spray it with low-calorie cooking spray, add the vegetables and fry over a medium-high heat for 5–8 minutes until softening. Add the spices and fry for a further 2 minutes until fragrant, then add everything else to the pan, reduce the heat right down and simmer for 25–30 minutes until the vegetables are cooked and sauce thickened. Add the lime juice and cream cheese and stir to combine. Season with salt to taste and serve.

LAMB *and* BARLEY CASSEROLE

🕐 **15 MINS**   🍲 **1 HR 40MINS**   ✕ **SERVES 4**

PER SERVING:
380 KCAL /34G CARBS

SPECIAL EQUIPMENT
Deep casserole dish with a tight-fitting lid (about 28cm/11in) suitable for oven and hob

low-calorie cooking spray
500g lean diced lamb
1 onion, peeled and diced
1 small leek, trimmed and sliced
250g carrots, peeled and cut into 1cm (½in)-thick slices
200g swede, peeled and cut into 1cm (½in) dice
1 tsp dried rosemary
1 x 400g tin chopped tomatoes
800ml meat stock (1 lamb or beef stock cube dissolved in 800ml boiling water)
1 tbsp Henderson's relish
2 dried bay leaves
100g pearl barley
sea salt and freshly ground black pepper

It's no secret that lamb and fragrant rosemary is a match made in heaven, and that's exactly why you'll find both in this fragrant casserole dish! To get our lean diced lamb chunks extra tender and juicy, we've simmered them with rosemary-infused chopped tomatoes, piping hot lamb stock and a glug of Hendo's. Once your onion, leek and swede are softened and naturally sweet, it's time to add your grains. A great alternative to potatoes, we stir in fibre-rich, nutritious pearl barley.

Everyday Light ────────────

Preheat the oven to 180°C (fan 160°C/gas mark 4).

Spray the casserole dish with low-calorie cooking spray and place over a medium-high heat. When the pan is hot, add the lamb and cook for 5 minutes, until sealed and well browned. Remove from the pan and set aside.

Give the pan another spritz with low-calorie cooking spray (no need to clean) and add the onion, leek, carrots and swede. Cook for 5 minutes until softened and golden.

Return the lamb to the pan. Add the rosemary, tomatoes, stock and Henderson's relish and bring to the boil. Pop in the bay leaves, cover with the lid and place in the oven to cook for 30 minutes.

After 30 minutes, remove from the oven and stir in the barley. Reduce the oven temperature to 160°C (fan 140°C/gas mark 3), replace the lid and return to the oven for 1 hour. When cooked, the vegetables should be soft, the lamb tender and the barley soft but with a slight bite. If it needs longer, return the dish to the oven, adding a little extra water if it looks like drying out. Taste and season with salt and pepper, if needed, and remove the bay leaves. Serve.

The casserole will keep in the fridge for up to 3 days.

TIP:
If you've frozen the casserole, when reheating after defrosting, you may need to add a splash of water or stock if it has dried out a little in the freezer.

MEDITERRANEAN-STYLE CHICKEN STEW *with* FETA DUMPLINGS

🕐 **15 MINS**   🍲 **1 HR 5 MINS**   ✕ **SERVES 4**

PER SERVING:
483 KCAL /50G CARBS

low-calorie cooking spray
500g skinless, boneless
  chicken thighs (visible fat
  removed), diced
1 onion, peeled and diced
4 garlic cloves, peeled and
  crushed
1 tsp dried oregano
2 peppers (mixed colours),
  deseeded and diced
1 courgette, cut into 1cm
  (½in)-thick half moons
3 tbsp tomato puree
1 x 400g tin chopped tomatoes
750ml chicken stock (1 chicken
  stock cube dissolved in 750ml
  boiling water)
1 x 400g tin butter beans, drained
12 pitted black olives, halved

FOR THE DUMPLINGS
150g self-raising flour
1 tsp baking powder
50g reduced-fat feta cheese,
  crumbled
handful of flat-leaf parsley,
  chopped
150g fat-free Greek yoghurt
sea salt and freshly ground
  black pepper

This chicken stew is too good to save for cold, wintery days. With tangy olives, creamy butter beans and salty feta in the mix, our Mediterranean-inspired recipe fills your bowl with holiday flavours, any time of year! You'll be obsessed with how fluffy the feta dumplings are – they're made with fat-free yoghurt, rather than suet, so they're lovely and light, and low in calories too.

Weekly Indulgence

Spray a large saucepan with low-calorie cooking spray and place over a medium heat. When hot, add the diced chicken and onion and fry for 10 minutes, until the chicken is well sealed and the onions have started to soften. Add the garlic and oregano and cook for a further minute, until fragrant, then add the peppers and courgette. Stir in the tomato puree, chopped tomatoes and stock. Bring to the boil, then reduce the heat to a simmer. Cover with a lid and cook for 30 minutes.

While the stew cooks, make the dumplings. Add the flour, baking powder, feta, half the chopped parsley and a pinch each of salt and pepper to a mixing bowl and stir well.

Add the yoghurt and gently stir until a dough forms. Don't knead and be careful not to overwork the dough as this can produce tough dumplings. Shape into 4 or 8 dumplings and cover until the stew is ready.

After 30 minutes, stir the butter beans and olives into the stew. When it starts to bubble again, place the dumplings on top, cover and cook for a further 20–25 minutes, until they are risen and fluffy and a skewer comes out clean when inserted into the middle.

Sprinkle with the remaining parsley and serve.

The stew and dumplings will keep in the fridge for up to 3 days.

ONE-POT QUINOA CHILLI

🕐 **15 MINS**   🍲 **45 MINS**   ✕ **SERVES 4**

USE GF STOCK
CUBES AND
OMIT THE
MARMITE

PER SERVING:
325 KCAL /48G CARBS

low-calorie cooking spray
1 onion, peeled and chopped
2 peppers (mixed colours),
  deseeded and chopped
1 courgette, grated
1 large carrot, peeled and grated
4 garlic cloves, peeled and
  crushed
1 red or green chilli, finely
  chopped (remove seeds if you
  prefer a milder chilli)
1 tsp dried herbes de Provence
1 tsp chilli powder (mild or hot,
  depending on your preference)
2 tsp ground cumin
1 tsp smoked paprika
2 tbsp tomato puree
1 x 400g tin chopped tomatoes
600ml vegetable stock
  (2 vegetable stock cubes
  dissolved in 600ml boiling
  water)
3 tbsp Henderson's relish or
  vegetarian Worcestershire
  sauce
2 tsp Marmite
juice of 1 lime
150g sweet potato, peeled and
  cut into 1cm (½in) dice
75g quinoa, rinsed
1 x 400g tin mixed beans, drained
  and rinsed
150g sweetcorn (tinned, or frozen
  and cooked)
large bunch of fresh coriander,
  roughly chopped
lime wedges, to serve (*optional*)

TO ACCOMPANY
75g mixed salad (+ 15 kcal per
  serving)

Vegan and dairy-free, this quinoa chilli is sure to keep everyone at the table happy. Inspired by the convenience of microwave meals, we've kept prep to a minimum, so you can relax and let this simmer until ready to serve. With high-protein tinned beans, quinoa and plenty of vegetables, it'll leave you feeling full all on its own. If you're feeling really hungry, serve it with rice or a wholemeal bread roll to mop up what's left. Like most chilli recipes, it tastes even better the next day.

Everyday Light

Spray a large saucepan with low-calorie cooking spray and place over a medium heat. Add the onion, peppers, courgette, carrot, garlic and chopped chilli and fry for 8–10 minutes, until the vegetables are softened. Add the dried herbs, chilli powder, cumin and smoked paprika and cook for a minute, until fragrant, then stir in the tomato puree, chopped tomatoes, stock, Henderson's relish, Marmite and lime juice. Increase the heat and bring to the boil, cover with a tight-fitting lid and reduce the heat to a simmer. Cook for 10 minutes.

Stir in the sweet potato and quinoa, replace the lid and cook for another 20 minutes, stirring once or twice.

After 20 minutes, stir in the beans and sweetcorn and cook for another 5 minutes until thoroughly heated through. Stir in the chopped coriander and add the lime wedges to the side, if using. Serve with some mixed salad, if you like: we've suggested this accompaniment to ensure this is a true, all-in-one recipe. You can enjoy this dish with any accompaniment you like, but don't forget to adjust the calories accordingly.

The dish will keep in the fridge for up to 3 days.

FULL ENGLISH CASSEROLE

🕐 **15 MINS**   🍲 **40 MINS**   ✕ **SERVES 4**

PER SERVING:
360 KCAL /32G CARBS

SPECIAL EQUIPMENT
Shallow casserole dish with a tight-fitting lid (about 28cm/11in), suitable for oven and hob

low-calorie cooking spray
4 reduced-fat pork sausages
½ onion, peeled and thinly sliced
4 bacon medallions, cut into 1.5cm (¾in)-thick strips
100g chestnut mushrooms, quartered
½ tsp garlic granules
200g passata
200ml water
200g new potatoes, cut into thin slices
1 x 420g tin baked beans
8 cherry tomatoes, halved
1 tbsp Henderson's relish or Worcestershire sauce
50g baby spinach leaves
4 medium eggs
freshly ground black pepper
handful of flat-leaf parsley, roughly chopped, to serve

TO ACCOMPANY
1 medium slice wholemeal toast, 37g (+ 84 kcal per serving)

A hearty cooked breakfast is always a good start to the day, but it can often leave a massive pile of washing-up afterwards! To cut down on pots and pans, we've taken inspiration from the all-in-one Middle Eastern-style dish shakshuka, except we've left out the spices to make our version nice and mild. Underneath the tomatoey baked eggs, you'll find all the most delicious bits of a Full English, from sausage, bacon and mushrooms to sliced new potatoes and even baked beans.

Everyday Light _____

Spray the casserole dish with low-calorie cooking spray and place over a medium heat. Add the sausages and onion and cook for 6–8 minutes until nicely browned, then add the bacon, mushrooms and garlic granules and cook for 2 minutes. Add the passata, water and potato slices, bring to the boil, then reduce the heat, cover and simmer for 15 minutes.

Stir in the baked beans, cherry tomatoes and Henderson's relish or Worcestershire sauce, bring back to a bubble, replace the lid and cook for a further 5 minutes or until the potatoes are just cooked. Stir in the spinach until wilted.

Use the back of a spoon to make 4 depressions in the mixture and carefully crack an egg into each, season with pepper and replace the lid. Cook for 6–9 minutes, until the egg whites have set and the yolks are cooked to your liking.

Remove from the heat, remove the lid, sprinkle with chopped parsley and serve!

ONE-POT SAUSAGE BOLOGNESE

🕐 **15 MINS**   🍲 **45 MINS**   ✕ **SERVES 4**

PER SERVING:
431 KCAL /59G CARBS

SPECIAL EQUIPMENT
Large, deep sauté pan or frying pan with lid

low-calorie cooking spray
1 onion, peeled and finely diced
2 carrots, peeled and finely diced
2 celery sticks, finely diced
2 garlic cloves, peeled and crushed
400g pack reduced-fat pork sausages, meat squeezed out of the skins and skins discarded
2 tsp dried oregano
2 tbsp tomato puree
500g passata
1 red wine (or chicken) stock pot
1 tbsp Henderson's relish or Worcestershire sauce
500ml boiling water
200g dried spaghetti
freshly ground black pepper
basil leaves, to garnish (*optional*)

TIPS:

Make sure you cut the vegetables small for this recipe. This will help keep the spaghetti from clumping together.

If you've frozen the bolognese, when reheating after defrosting, you may need to add a splash of water if it has dried out a little in the freezer.

Once you try this all-in-one spag bol, there's no going back to a hob full of pots and pans! Rather than the usual beef mince, we've used reduced-fat pork sausages as the meat for this bolognese. As well as keeping the calories nice and low, the sausages cook really quickly, so you can add your spaghetti straight to the pan, leave everything to simmer together, and be ready to serve dinner, all in less than an hour.

Weekly Indulgence

Spray the deep sauté pan or frying pan with low-calorie cooking spray and place over a medium heat. Add the onion, carrots, celery and garlic and fry for 10–12 minutes, until soft and golden. Add the sausage meat and cook for 5 minutes, breaking up the meat with a wooden spoon, until browned. Add the oregano, tomato puree, passata, stock pot and Henderson's relish or Worcestershire sauce. Stir well and bring to the boil, then reduce the heat, cover and simmer for 15 minutes.

Add the boiling water and spaghetti to the pan (you can break the spaghetti in half to make it easier). Stir well, until all the spaghetti is separated and well mixed into the sauce. It will look a little watery, but don't worry, the spaghetti will absorb the liquid as it cooks, and the sauce will thicken.

When the sauce starts to bubble, replace the lid and cook for 12 minutes, stirring halfway through.

Season with pepper and serve, garnished with basil leaves, if using.

The bolognese will keep in the fridge for up to 3 days.

SAUSAGE *and* LENTIL STEW

🕐 **15 MINS**   🍲 **50 MINS**   ✕ **SERVES 4**

VEGGIE

USE VEGGIE
SAUSAGES AND
STOCK

VEGAN

USE VEGAN
SAUSAGES AND
STOCK

FREEZE
ME

BATCH
COOK

DAIRY
FREE

GLUTEN
FREE

USE GF
SAUSAGES AND
STOCK CUBE

PER SERVING:
324 KCAL / 38G CARBS

SPECIAL EQUIPMENT
28cm (11in) non-stick shallow
   casserole dish or sauté pan
   with tight-fitting lid

low-calorie cooking spray
8 reduced-fat pork sausages
2 onions, peeled and diced
2 celery sticks, thinly sliced
200g carrots, peeled and
   thinly sliced
2 garlic cloves, peeled and
   crushed
3 tbsp tomato puree
500ml chicken stock (1 chicken
   stock cube dissolved in 500ml
   boiling water)
1 eating apple, peeled and diced
1 tbsp fresh thyme leaves
   (or 1 tsp dried)
2 dried bay leaves
2 x 400g tins green lentils in
   water, drained and rinsed
1 tbsp balsamic vinegar
sea salt and freshly ground black
   pepper

TO ACCOMPANY
60g wholemeal bread roll
   (+ 146 kcal per serving)

When you fancy a no-frills comfort dish, our Sausage and Lentil Stew is ideal. Made with nothing but budget-friendly staples, this one-dish wonder teams protein-packed green lentils with a classic casserole base of onions, carrots and celery. To keep the calories down without compromising on heartiness, we use reduced-fat pork sausages. Brought to life with garlic, thyme, balsamic vinegar and juicy apple slices, you'll love coming back to it on busy days – don't forget to stash leftovers in the freezer!

Everyday Light

Spray the casserole dish or sauté pan with low-calorie cooking spray and place over a medium-high heat. Add the sausages and cook for about 5 minutes until browned. Remove them from the casserole dish and put to one side. They don't need to be fully cooked as you will add them back to the casserole dish shortly.

Reduce the heat to medium and add the onions, celery and carrots to the casserole dish. Cook for 6–8 minutes until the onions are softening and beginning to turn golden, then add the garlic and tomato puree and cook for a further minute. Stir in the stock, diced apple and thyme. Return the sausages to the casserole dish and add the bay leaves. Bring to the boil, then reduce the heat to a simmer. Cover and cook for 30 minutes or until the vegetables are tender.

Stir in the lentils and balsamic vinegar and turn up the heat and bring back to a simmer. Cook for another 5 minutes, until the lentils are piping hot. Remove the bay leaves, taste and season with salt and pepper, if required. Serve, with a wholemeal bread roll if you like: we've suggested this accompaniment to ensure this is a true, all-in-one recipe. You can enjoy this dish with any accompaniment you like, but don't forget to adjust the calories accordingly.

The stew will keep in the fridge for up to 3 days.

TIP:

If you've frozen the stew, when reheating after defrosting, you may need to add a splash of water if it has dried out a little.

SLOW COOKER CREAMY SAUSAGE *and* BEAN CASSEROLE

🕐 **5 MINS**   🍲 **3½–6½ HOURS**   ✕ **SERVES 4**

PER SERVING:
347 KCAL /37G CARBS

SPECIAL EQUIPMENT
3.5-litre slow cooker

low-calorie cooking spray
8 reduced-fat pork sausages
1 onion, peeled and sliced
1 leek, trimmed and sliced
4 garlic cloves, peeled and
    crushed
600ml chicken or vegetable
    stock (1 chicken or vegetable
    stock cube dissolved in 600ml
    boiling water)
2 tbsp cornflour, mixed to a
    slurry with 2 tbsp water
75g reduced-fat cream cheese
25g Parmesan, finely grated
2 x 400g tins cannellini beans in
    water, drained and rinsed
freshly ground black pepper
handful of fresh basil leaves,
    chopped, to serve

TO ACCOMPANY *(optional)*
60g wholemeal bread roll
    (+ 146 kcal per roll)

TIP:

We prefer to brown the
sausages first, as it improves
the texture and makes them
look more appealing, but if
you are pushed for time you
can add them straight to
the pot!

We'll never turn down a sausage casserole, and this one's
no exception! We've cooked everything in a rich, creamy
sauce with sweet slow-cooked onions and leeks, and
added a scrummy Italian-inspired twist with a sprinkling
of Parmesan and fresh basil. You'll definitely need a crusty
wholemeal bread roll on standby, to help you mop up
every last drop of sauce! Bear in mind that you can skip
browning your sausages first, if you're short on time – we
like to do it because we find it makes the whole dish look
even more delicious.

Everyday Light

Spray a frying pan with low-calorie cooking spray and fry
the sausages over a medium-high heat for about 5 minutes,
until nicely browned.

Place the onion, leek and garlic in the slow cooker pot,
add the stock and cornflour slurry and stir well. Add the
browned sausages to the pot, cover with the lid and cook
on low for 5–6 hours or on high for 3–4 hours.

After 3–4/5–6 hours, stir in the cream cheese until melted,
and add the Parmesan and cannellini beans. Re-cover with
the lid and leave for a further 30 minutes, until the beans are
thoroughly heated through.

Season with black pepper, to taste, and stir in the basil just
before serving.

IF YOU DON'T HAVE A SLOW COOKER
Alternatively, cook this on the hob in a large pan with a
tight-fitting lid. Spray the inside of the pan with a little
low-calorie cooking spray and brown the sausages over a
medium-high heat, then fry the onions, leeks and garlic for
5 minutes. Add the stock and cornflour slurry. Bring to the
boil, cover with a tight-fitting lid and simmer for 35 minutes.
Add the beans, stir in the cream cheese and Parmesan, and
cook for a further 5 minutes until the beans are thoroughly
heated through. Season with black pepper and stir in the
basil just before serving.

FAKEAWAYS

FREEZE
ME

BATCH
COOK

DAIRY
FREE

USE DF
CREAM CHEESE

GLUTEN
FREE

USE GF
STOCK CUBE

FRUITY CHICKEN CURRY

🕐 **20 MINS**   🍲 **1 HR**   ✕ **SERVES 4**

PER SERVING:
339 KCAL /26G CARBS

SPECIAL EQUIPMENT
Large, deep frying pan or shallow casserole dish with lid (about 28cm/11in), suitable for hob

low-calorie cooking spray
600g skinless, boneless chicken thighs (visible fat removed), cut into large chunks
1 medium onion, peeled and finely diced
4 garlic cloves, peeled and crushed
3cm (1¼in) piece of root ginger, peeled and finely grated
1 medium red chilli, deseeded and finely chopped
1 ripe mango, skin and stone removed, cut into 2cm (¾in) chunks (about 200g chunks)
200g fresh ripe pineapple, cut into 1–2cm (½–¾in) chunks and thinly sliced
1 eating apple, skin and core removed, cut into 1cm (½in) dice
2 tbsp mild curry powder
400ml coconut plant-based drink
1 chicken stock cube, crumbled
1 tsp fresh lime juice
2 tbsp reduced-fat cream cheese
sea salt and freshly ground black pepper

TO ACCOMPANY
50g mini naan bread (+ 127 kcal per naan)

You've not experienced true convenience until you've made a curry in a casserole dish! This Fruity Chicken Curry cuts down on faff and turns up the flavour, with mango, pineapple and apple: the blend of natural, fruity sweetness and medium-hot spices makes this a crowd-pleaser that everyone will want to try. To get things nice and creamy while keeping the calories low, we've swapped coconut milk for a plant-based coconut drink, and it works like a charm! The lime juice adds an invigorating, citrusy lift.

Weekly Indulgence ────────────

Spray the large shallow casserole dish or frying pan with low-calorie cooking spray and place over a medium-high heat.

When the casserole dish is hot, add the chicken and fry for about 5 minutes, turning, until browned on all sides. Remove from the casserole dish and set aside.

Lower the heat to medium, add the onion and fry for 5 minutes until soft and golden. Add the garlic, ginger and chilli and cook for a further 1–2 minutes. Add the mango, pineapple and apple and cook for about 5 minutes, until the fruit is softening and golden. Add the curry powder and continue cooking for 1–2 minutes, until fragrant.

Add the browned chicken, coconut drink and crumbled stock cube to the pan and stir well. Bring to the boil, then reduce the heat, cover and simmer for 35–40 minutes, until the fruit is soft, the chicken is cooked through and the sauce has thickened.

Stir in the lime juice and remove from the heat. Add the cream cheese and stir in until completely blended. Season to taste with salt and pepper, if needed. Serve with a mini naan bread: we've used this accompaniment to ensure this is a true, all-in-one recipe. You can enjoy this dish with any accompaniment you like, but don't forget to adjust the calories accordingly.

The curry will keep in the fridge for up to 2 days.

KORAI-STYLE CHICKEN CURRY

🕐 **20 MINS**   🍲 **VARIABLE**   ✕ **SERVES 4**

PER SERVING:
268 KCAL /16G CARBS

low-calorie cooking spray
2 medium onions, peeled and chopped
1 medium red pepper, deseeded and cut into 2cm (¾in) dice
1 medium green pepper, deseeded and cut into 2cm (¾in) dice
4 garlic cloves, peeled and crushed
2cm (¾in) piece of root ginger, peeled and finely chopped
1 small red chilli, deseeded and finely chopped
600g skinless, boneless chicken thighs (visible fat removed), cut into 3cm (1in) chunks
1 tbsp garam masala
1 tsp ground turmeric
1 tsp mild chilli powder
1 tsp ground coriander
1 tsp ground cumin
1 x 400g tin chopped tomatoes
1 tbsp tomato puree
500ml chicken stock (250ml for slow and pressure cooker methods) (1 reduced-salt chicken stock cube dissolved in 500/250ml boiling water)
juice of ½ lemon
½ tsp salt
½ tsp white granulated sweetener or granulated sugar
3 tbsp roughly chopped fresh coriander leaves, to garnish (*optional*)

TO ACCOMPANY
50g mini naan bread (+ 127 kcal per naan)

Similar to a Balti, our Korai-style Chicken Curry is a medium-hot dish of tender chicken, juicy peppers and fragrant spices. We've given you the option of cooking it in the oven, slow cooker or pressure cooker, so you can have it ready when it best suits you. As tasty as a takeaway, for a fraction of the calories, we reckon it's best served with a warm, soft, mini naan to mop up the spicy tomato sauce.

Everyday Light ————————————————

HOB-TOP METHOD
🍲 **1 HOUR 45 MINS–2 HOURS 15 MINS**

SPECIAL EQUIPMENT
Large casserole dish with tight-fitting lid (about 26cm/10in), suitable for hob and oven

Preheat the oven to 190°C (fan 170°C/gas mark 5).

Spray the casserole dish with low-calorie cooking spray and place over a medium heat. Add the onion, peppers, garlic, ginger and red chilli, stir well and cook for 10 minutes until the onions are soft and golden. Add the chicken, garam masala, turmeric, chilli powder, ground coriander and cumin, stir well and cook for 3–4 minutes, until the chicken is sealed on all sides. Stir in the chopped tomatoes, tomato puree, chicken stock, lemon juice, salt and sweetener, cover with a tight-fitting lid and cook in the oven for 1½–2 hours until the chicken is cooked and the sauce has reduced and thickened. Check halfway through to make sure the curry is not drying out, adding a little water if needed.

Remove from the oven, sprinkle with chopped coriander to garnish (if using) and serve with a mini naan bread. We've suggested this accompaniment to ensure this is a true, all-in-one recipe. You can enjoy this dish with any accompaniment you like, but don't forget to adjust the calories accordingly.

The curry will keep, covered, in the fridge for up to 2 days.

FAKEAWAYS

PRESSURE-COOKER METHOD
🍲 45 MINS

SPECIAL EQUIPMENT
Pressure cooker

Spray the inside of the pressure cooker with low-calorie cooking spray and set to sauté. Add the onion, peppers, garlic, ginger and red chilli, stir well and cook for 10 minutes until the onions are softening and golden. Add the chicken, garam masala, turmeric, chilli powder, ground coriander and cumin, stir well and cook for 3–4 minutes until the chicken is sealed on all sides. Stir in the chopped tomatoes, tomato puree, chicken stock, lemon juice, salt and sweetener or sugar, close the lid and lock. Set to pressure cook, high, and set the timer for 30 minutes.

After 30 minutes cooking, release the pressure using natural pressure release.

When the float valve has gone down, open the lid. Sauté with the lid off for a few more minutes, until the sauce has reduced and thickened. Sprinkle with chopped coriander to garnish (if using) and serve with a mini naan bread. We've suggested this accompaniment to ensure this is a true, all-in-one recipe. You can enjoy this dish with any accompaniment you like, but don't forget to adjust the calories accordingly.

The curry will keep, covered, in the fridge for up to 2 days.

SLOW-COOKER METHOD
🍲 4 HOURS 15 MINS–5 HOURS 15 MINS

SPECIAL EQUIPMENT
3.5-litre slow cooker

If your slow cooker has a sauté function, spray with low-calorie cooking spray, add the onion, peppers, garlic, ginger and red chilli, stir well and sauté for 10 minutes until the onions are softening and golden. Add the chicken, garam masala, turmeric, chilli powder, ground coriander and cumin, stir well and cook for 3–4 minutes until the chicken is sealed on all sides. If there is no sauté function, you will have to cook the ingredients in a frying pan and transfer it to the slow cooker. Stir in the chopped tomatoes, tomato puree, chicken stock, lemon juice, salt and sweetener or sugar, cover with the lid and cook on high for 4–5 hours.

Remove the lid and cook for a few more minutes until reduced and thickened.

Sprinkle with chopped coriander to garnish (if using) and serve with a mini naan bread.

We've suggested this accompaniment to ensure this is a true, all-in-one recipe. You can enjoy this dish with any accompaniment you like, but don't forget to adjust the calories accordingly.

The curry will keep, covered, in the fridge for up to 2 days.

TIPS:

The optional coriander garnish will add an additional 1 kcal per portion.

If you'd like to increase the chilli heat in this curry, try leaving the seeds in the red chilli.

FAKEAWAYS

VEGGIE

VEGAN

FREEZE ME

BATCH COOK

DAIRY FREE

GLUTEN FREE

USE GF STOCK CUBE AND NAAN BREAD

YELLOW PEA *and* SWEET POTATO CURRY

🕐 **15 MINS** 🍲 **55 MINS** ✕ **SERVES 4**

PER SERVING:
273 KCAL /31G CARBS

low-calorie cooking spray
1 tbsp fenugreek seeds
1 onion, peeled and finely diced
2 carrots, peeled and finely diced
3 garlic cloves, peeled and crushed
5cm (2in) piece of root ginger, peeled and grated
1 tbsp garam masala
½ tsp ground turmeric
250g yellow split peas, rinsed
2 tbsp tomato puree
1 x 400ml tin light coconut milk
450ml vegetable stock (1 vegetable stock cube dissolved in 450ml boiling water)
250g sweet potatoes, peeled and cut into 1cm (½in) dice
juice of ½ lime
handful of fresh coriander, roughly chopped
80g spinach
sea salt and freshly ground black pepper

TO ACCOMPANY
50g mini naan bread (+ 127 kcal per naan)

TIP:
If you can't get hold of fenugreek seeds, you can replace them with 1 tsp of ground fenugreek, added with the garam masala and other spices or 1 tbsp fenugreek leaves, added with the stock

Fragrant and mild, this easy, budget-friendly curry will have you counting down the days until your next fakeaway night! As well as being vegan and dairy free, it brings a lovely aromatic flavour to the table that the whole family will enjoy. Yellow split peas are cheap and cheerful and are always worth having in the cupboard. Rich with gentle spices, hearty sweet potato and creamy coconut milk, make sure you serve this dish with a fluffy mini naan to mop up every last bit.

Everyday Light

Spray a large saucepan with low-calorie cooking spray and place over a medium heat. Add the fenugreek seeds and toast for 1–2 minutes, stirring all the time to prevent them catching, then add the onion and carrots and cook for 5 minutes, until the onions begin to soften. Add the garlic, ginger, garam masala and turmeric and cook for 1 minute until fragrant, then stir in the yellow split peas, tomato puree, coconut milk and stock. Turn the heat to high and bring to the boil. Reduce the heat to a simmer, cover with a lid and cook for 15 minutes.

After 15 minutes, add the sweet potatoes and stir well. Replace the lid and continue cooking for 30 minutes, stirring once or twice to prevent sticking.

Test the peas, to make sure they are cooked. They should have absorbed most of the liquid and be soft, but still holding their shape. If your peas are older, they may take a little longer to cook. Test every 5 minutes until they are cooked to your liking and add a splash of water if it becomes dry.

Stir in the lime juice, coriander and spinach and cook until just wilted. Season with salt and pepper and serve with mini naan bread: we've used this accompaniment to ensure this is a true, all-in-one recipe. You can enjoy this dish with any accompaniment you like, but don't forget to adjust the calories accordingly.

The curry will keep in the fridge for up to 3 days.

FAKEAWAYS

FREEZE ME

BATCH COOK

DAIRY FREE

USE DF CREAM CHEESE

GLUTEN FREE

LAMB PASANDA

🕐 **15 MINS**　　🍲 **VARIABLE**　　✕ **SERVES 4**

PER SERVING:
402 KCAL /15G CARBS

low-calorie cooking spray
2 medium red onions, peeled and finely chopped
4 garlic cloves, peeled and crushed
2cm (¾in) piece of root ginger, peeled and finely chopped
1 small red chilli, deseeded and finely chopped
500g diced lean leg of lamb, any visible fat removed
1 tbsp garam masala
1 tsp ground turmeric
1 tsp ground cumin
1 tsp ground coriander
½ tsp mild chilli powder
600ml coconut plant-based drink
2 tbsp ground almonds
½ tsp salt
½ tsp white granulated sweetener or granulated sugar
2 tbsp reduced-fat cream cheese

TO GARNISH (*optional*)
1 tbsp toasted flaked almonds
1 tbsp roughly chopped fresh coriander leaves

TO ACCOMPANY
50g mini naan bread
(+ 127 kcal per naan. We've suggested this accompaniment to ensure this is a true, all-in-one recipe. You can enjoy this dish with any accompaniment but don't forget to adjust the calories accordingly.

Our aromatic, luxuriously creamy Lamb Pasanda is jam-packed with restaurant-inspired flavours. It uses simple, easy to find ingredients, is mildly spiced and includes an irresistible crunchy, toasted flaked almond topping! Make sure you use reduced-fat cream cheese instead of low-fat cream cheese, so that your leftovers will freeze and reheat without losing the velvety deliciousness of fresh portions.

Special Occasion ──────────────

OVEN METHOD
🍲 **2–2¼ HOURS**

SPECIAL EQUIPMENT
Casserole dish with tight-fitting lid (about 26cm/10in), suitable for oven and hob

Preheat the oven to 180°C (fan 160°C/gas mark 4).

Spray the casserole dish with low-calorie cooking spray and place over a medium heat. Add the onion, garlic, ginger and red chilli and fry gently for 5–10 minutes, stirring, until softened. Add the diced lamb, garam masala, ground turmeric, ground cumin, ground coriander and chilli powder, stir well and fry gently for 2–3 minutes until the lamb is sealed on all sides. Add the coconut plant-based drink, ground almonds, salt and sweetener or sugar and stir well.

Cover with a tight-fitting lid and cook in the oven for 1½–2 hours, stirring halfway through, until the lamb is very tender and the sauce has reduced and thickened.

Remove from the oven and stir in the cream cheese until completely blended. Scatter a few toasted flaked almonds and chopped coriander on top, if using, and serve with a mini naan bread.

The pasanda will keep in the fridge for up to 3 days.

FAKEAWAYS

SLOW-COOKER METHOD
3¼–4¼ HOURS

SPECIAL EQUIPMENT
3.5-litre slow cooker

If your slow cooker has a sauté function, spray with low-calorie cooking spray and sauté the onion, garlic, ginger and red chilli gently for 5–10 minutes, stirring, until softened.

Add the diced lamb, garam masala, ground turmeric, ground cumin, ground coriander and chilli powder, stir well and fry gently for 2–3 minutes until the lamb is sealed on all sides. If there is no sauté function, you will have to do the first steps in a frying pan and transfer it to the slow cooker.

Add the coconut plant-based drink, ground almonds, salt and sweetener or sugar and stir well. Cover with the lid and cook on high for 3–4 hours, until the lamb is very tender and the sauce has reduced and thickened.

Turn off the slow cooker and stir in the cream cheese until completely blended. If you're using toasted flaked almonds and chopped coriander leaves, sprinkle a few on top and serve with a mini naan bread.

The pasanda will keep in the fridge for up to 3 days.

TIPS:

This recipe is mild to medium in heat – add a little more chilli powder if you'd prefer it hotter.

You can buy ready-toasted flaked almonds for convenience, rather than toasting your own.

We've included an optional garnish of flaked toasted almonds and 1 tbsp of chopped coriander leaves. This will add an additional 13 kcal to each portion of the dish.

CHILLI CHICKEN MASALA

🕐 **15 MINS***   🍲 **30 MINS**   ✕ **SERVES 6**

*PLUS 10 MINS MARINATING

PER SERVING:
198 KCAL /11G CARBS

650g chicken breast, diced
1 tbsp ground turmeric
1 tbsp ground coriander
1 tbsp ground cumin
1 tsp garam masala
1 tsp paprika
1 tsp curry powder
1 tsp medium chilli powder
½ tsp dried chilli flakes
low-calorie cooking spray
1 medium onion, peeled and diced
1 green pepper, deseeded and
   diced
1 red pepper, deseeded and
   diced
2 green chillies, deseeded and
   finely chopped
2 garlic cloves, peeled and
   crushed
5cm (2in) piece of root ginger,
   peeled and finely grated
1 x 400g tin chopped tomatoes
2 tbsp tomato puree
2 tsp hot pepper sauce
200ml boiling water
1 chicken stock pot
100g fat-free plain yoghurt
handful of fresh coriander
   leaves, chopped

TO ACCOMPANY
50g mini naan bread
   (+ 127 kcal per naan)

TIPS:

This is quite a hot curry, but if you
want it even hotter add a little
more hot sauce or an extra chilli.

You can marinate the chicken for
longer to give it a more intense
flavour.

Our Chilli Chicken Masala packs a punch when it comes to
fakeaway flavour, thanks to the chillies, ginger and glug
of hot sauce. Perfect for warming you up as the nights get
colder, it takes just half an hour of simmering to make a
curry that'll give your local restaurant a run for its money.
And it's ideal for batch cooking, so you can have a few
portions stashed in the freezer for days when you really
don't want to wait for dinner!

Everyday Light ─────────────

Put the chicken in a mixing bowl and add all the ground,
dried spices, including the curry powder, chilli powder and
chilli flakes, then stir until fully coated. Cover the bowl with
cling film and pop in the fridge for 10 minutes to allow the
chicken to marinate.

Spray a large frying pan with low-calorie cooking spray
and place over a medium heat. Add the marinated chicken
and any excess marinade to the pan and fry for 4 minutes
until browned on all sides, then add the onion and fry
for another 5 minutes until just starting to soften. Add the
peppers and green chillies and fry for a further 2 minutes
and when the peppers and onion are soft, add the garlic
and ginger and pour in the chopped tomatoes, tomato
puree and hot pepper sauce, stirring until combined. Pour in
the boiling water, add the stock pot and stir until dissolved,
then simmer for 20 minutes.

Stir through the yoghurt and chopped coriander and serve
with a mini naan bread: we've used this accompaniment
to ensure this is a true, all-in-one recipe. You can enjoy this
dish with any accompaniment you like, but don't forget to
adjust the calories accordingly.

The dish keeps in the fridge for up to 3 days.

FREEZE ME

BATCH COOK

DAIRY FREE

USE DF YOGHURT

GLUTEN FREE

USE GF STOCK POT

ONE-POT CHICKEN TIKKA *and* RICE

🕐 **20 MINS***   🍲 **45 MINS**   ✕ **SERVES 4**

*PLUS 30 MINS MARINATING

PER SERVING:
497 KCAL /65G CARBS

SPECIAL EQUIPMENT
28cm (11in) shallow casserole dish with tight-fitting lid, suitable for oven and hob

600g skinless boneless chicken thighs (visible fat removed), cut in half
low-calorie cooking spray
1 large onion, peeled and thinly sliced
2 red peppers, deseeded and thinly sliced
4 garlic cloves, peeled and crushed
4cm (1½in) piece of root ginger, peeled and grated
1 tbsp tikka curry powder
1 x 400g tin chopped tomatoes
400ml coconut plant-based drink
1 chicken stock pot
1 tbsp mango chutney
juice of ½ lemon
handful of fresh mint leaves, chopped
handful of fresh coriander leaves, chopped
225g basmati rice, rinsed

FOR THE MARINADE
1 tbsp tikka curry powder
75g fat-free Greek yoghurt

TO ACCOMPANY *(optional)*
1 tbsp fat-free Greek yoghurt (+ 26 kcal per tbsp)

Even easier than ordering takeaway, this all-in-one curry never disappoints. Just as the name suggests, there's no need to cook rice separately, so you'll have fewer pots to clean after your meal. The tikka-style sauce comes together in no time, using a plant-based coconut drink to make it lovely and creamy, without adding lots of calories. Once you've stirred in the rice, all that's left to do is sit the chicken on top, then pop everything into the oven.

Weekly Indulgence

Mix together the marinade ingredients in a bowl, add the chicken thigh pieces and mix to coat. Cover and marinate in the fridge for 30 minutes.

Preheat the oven to 200°C (fan 180°C/gas mark 6).

Spray the casserole dish with low-calorie cooking spray and place over a medium-high heat. When hot, add the marinated chicken thigh pieces and cook for 2 minutes on each side to brown. Remove from the pan and set to one side.

Lower the heat to medium and give the pan another spritz of low-calorie cooking spray if it needs it. Add the onion, peppers, garlic and ginger and fry for 6–8 minutes until soft, then add the tikka curry powder and cook for another minute. Add the tomatoes, coconut drink and stock pot (no need to dissolve it in water) and bring to the boil, then stir in the mango chutney, lemon juice and chopped herbs, saving a few to sprinkle on top at the end. Stir in the rice, then lay the chicken on top. Cover with the lid and place in the oven for 30 minutes.

Remove from the oven, sprinkle with the rest of the herbs and serve with a dollop of fat-free Greek yoghurt (if using).

The dish will keep in the fridge for 1–2 days.

FAKEAWAYS

TANDOORI-STYLE WHOLE CHICKEN *with* CUMIN-ROASTED VEGETABLES

🕐 **30 MINS***   🍲 **1 HR**   ✕ **SERVES 4**

*PLUS 1 HR MARINATING

PER SERVING:
694 KCAL /31G CARBS

SPECIAL EQUIPMENT
Extra-large baking tray, sharp kitchen scissors/shears

1 medium whole chicken, about 1.5kg
low-calorie cooking spray
sea salt and freshly ground black pepper
½ lemon, cut into wedges, to serve

FOR THE MARINADE
200g fat-free Greek yoghurt
1 tsp ground ginger
1 tsp ground cumin
1 tsp ground coriander
1 tsp sweet paprika
½ tsp cayenne pepper
½ tsp garlic powder
1 tsp salt
juice of ½ lemon

FOR THE VEGETABLES
300g baby potatoes, cut in half
300g baby carrots, peeled and cut in half lengthways
300g cauliflower, cut into florets
200g baby parsnips, peeled and cut in half lengthways
8 shallots, peeled and halved
8 garlic cloves, peeled
1 tsp ground cumin

Just imagine a plateful of this tender marinated chicken, baby potatoes and roasted vegetables in front of you – you'll feel like you're eating out, from the comfort of your own home! The trick is to let the tandoori-style marinade mingle overnight, to really let your chicken soak up the spices. Spatchcocking your chicken means it'll be on your plate sooner, with just as much flavour!

Special Occasion

Put all the marinade ingredients in a large bowl, mix well and set aside.

Place the chicken breast side down on a chopping board, with the legs pointing towards you. Starting at the leg end, cut right along one side of the backbone using sharp kitchen scissors. Spin the chicken around so the wings are pointing towards you and cut along the other side of the backbone. Remove the backbone and discard, or keep it to make some stock. Flip the chicken over and press down firmly on the breastbone to flatten it out. Remove as much of the skin and fat as possible, then make a few cuts across the breast and thick part of the legs so the marinade can be absorbed into the flesh.

Place the flattened chicken in the bowl with the marinade. Spoon the marinade over, making sure the whole chicken is well coated, cover the bowl and pop it in the fridge for at least 1 hour, preferably overnight.

After marinating, preheat the oven to 200°C (fan 180°C/gas mark 6).

Put the vegetables and garlic in a large bowl and spray with low-calorie cooking spray, sprinkle over the cumin and season with salt and pepper. Mix well until completely coated.

Line one third of an extra-large baking tray with a sheet of kitchen foil.

Remove the spatcocked chicken from the marinade and place it on the foil breast side up. Spray the unlined part of the baking tray with low-calorie cooking spray and add the vegetables. Spread the vegetables out evenly over the tray and place in the oven for about 45 minutes, turning the vegetables halfway through.

The chicken should be cooked through, its juices should run clear when a sharp knife is inserted into the thickest part, and it should show no sign of pinkness. The vegetables should be tender and starting to colour around the edges. If not, return to the oven for a further 10–15 minutes or until everything is cooked through.

Cut the chicken into quarters or slice it so you can serve some light and dark meat in each portion.

Serve immediately, with the roasted vegetables and lemon wedges.

The chicken and vegetables will keep in the fridge for up to 2 days.

TIPS:

Our recipe is medium-spicy, but if you're in the mood to turn things up a notch, add more cayenne pepper to the pot.

If freezing, cool quickly then divide the chicken and vegetables into separate portions.

Freeze the chicken and vegetables separately in individual freezerproof containers. Defrost thoroughly overnight in the fridge. Remove excess moisture from the defrosted vegetables before reheating.

The chicken and vegetables can be covered and reheated in the microwave until piping hot throughout.

FREEZE ME

BATCH COOK

LOW CARB

DAIRY FREE

USE DF CREAM CHEESE

GLUTEN FREE

USE GF STOCK CUBE

BRAZILIAN-STYLE PEANUT *and* LIME CHICKEN CURRY

🕐 **15 MINS***   🍲 **25 MINS**   ✕ **SERVES 4**

*PLUS 20 MINS MARINATING

PER SERVING:
257 KCAL / 7.3G CARBS

SPECIAL EQUIPMENT
Large frying pan, or casserole dish suitable for hob

2 garlic cloves, peeled and finely chopped or crushed
finely grated zest and juice of 1 lime (about 25ml)
finely grated zest and juice of 1 lemon (about 25ml)
500g chicken breast, cut into strips
low-calorie cooking spray
1 medium onion, peeled and finely diced
1 medium red chilli, deseeded and finely chopped
2cm (¾in) piece of root ginger, peeled and finely chopped
½ tsp ground turmeric
2 tbsp smooth peanut butter
1 tbsp tomato puree
100ml fish stock (1 fish stock cube dissolved in 100ml boiling water)
250ml coconut plant-based drink
150g peeled raw king prawns
1 tbsp roughly chopped fresh coriander
1 tbsp roughly chopped flat-leaf parsley
sea salt and freshly ground black pepper

TO ACCOMPANY
25g mini flatbread (+ 78 kcal per flatbread)

Inspired by a classic Brazilian curry called Xinxim, this dish is creamy and zingy in equal measure. We've swapped the crayfish in the traditional version for prawns, making the recipe easier for everyday cooking. The sauce is nutty and zesty, with a hint of chilli to cut through those intense flavours. It's surprisingly low in calories, perfect if you want to dish it up with rice, although we like to add a mini flatbread on the side to soak up all that glorious sauce.

Everyday Light

Put the garlic, lime zest and juice and the lemon zest and juice into a large bowl and stir well. Add the chicken and stir to make sure all the strips are well coated. Cover and pop in the fridge for 20 minutes to marinate.

Spray the large frying pan or hob-safe casserole dish with low-calorie cooking spray and place over a medium-high heat.

Remove the chicken from the bowl, leaving as much of the marinade behind as possible as we don't want to boil the chicken in excess marinade when we come to seal it.

Put the chicken strips in the frying pan or casserole dish and cook for about 5 minutes to seal the meat all over. Add the onion and cook for another 5 minutes, until soft but not coloured, then add the chilli, ginger and turmeric and cook for 2 minutes. Stir in the peanut butter, tomato puree, stock and coconut drink, bring to the boil, then turn down the heat and simmer for 5 minutes. Add the prawns and simmer for another 5 minutes, or until the prawns are pink and cooked through.

Season with salt and pepper, stir in half the chopped coriander and parsley and sprinkle the rest over the top to serve. Serve with a warm mini flatbread. We've suggested this accompaniment to ensure this is a true, all-in-one recipe. You can enjoy this dish with any accompaniment you like, but don't forget to adjust the calories accordingly. The curry will keep in the fridge for 1 day.

FAKEAWAYS

USE GF
SOY SAUCE

THAI-STYLE BASIL TOFU STIR-FRY

🕐 **20 MINS***   🍲 **25 MINS**   ✕ **SERVES 4**

*PLUS 30 MINS PRESSING

PER SERVING:
333 KCAL /33G CARBS

SPECIAL EQUIPMENT
Large, deep frying pan (about 28cm/11in) or non-stick wok

450g extra-firm tofu
low-calorie cooking spray
1 medium red chilli, deseeded and finely chopped
4 garlic cloves, peeled and crushed
2cm (¾in) piece of root ginger, peeled and finely grated
1 medium onion, peeled and finely chopped
½ medium red pepper, deseeded and thinly sliced
½ medium green pepper, deseeded and thinly sliced
80g fine green beans, trimmed and cut diagonally into 2cm (¾in) lengths
1 x 250g pouch ready-cooked microwave jasmine rice
60g fresh Thai or Italian basil leaves
sea salt and freshly ground black pepper

FOR THE SAUCE
4 tbsp dark soy sauce
juice of ½ lime
pinch of white granulated sweetener or granulated sugar

TIP:

Use extra-firm tofu in this recipe as it contains less liquid and has a 'meaty' texture which holds together well in a stir-fry.

Ideal for a meat-free Monday (or any day of the week!), this aromatic stir-fry contains everything you could want from a complete meal, including plenty of tasty veggies and filling, fluffy rice. Combining savoury soy sauce with zesty lime, it's a speedy flavour sensation you can take from wok to plate with ease. Pressing tofu takes time, but you don't want to skip that step – removing the moisture guarantees your plant-based 'mince' will absorb the flavours from the sauce, and hold a firmer, meatier texture.

Everyday Light ────────────

Drain the tofu and place it on a plate between several sheets of kitchen paper. Place a plate on top and weigh it down with a heavy object. Leave for 30 minutes to press out the excess liquid. After pressing, discard the kitchen paper and crumble the tofu into small pieces that resemble minced meat. Set aside.

Mix the sauce ingredients together in a small bowl and set aside.

Spray the large, deep frying pan or wok with low-calorie cooking spray and place over a medium-high heat. When the pan is hot, add the crumbled tofu and stir-fry for 8–10 minutes, stirring occasionally, until golden brown on all sides. Add the red chilli, garlic and ginger and stir-fry for 1–2 minutes, until fragrant, then add the onion, peppers and green beans and stir-fry for 5–7 minutes, stirring frequently, until softening slightly but still retaining their crispness and colour. Tip the jasmine rice from its pouch into a bowl and break it up with a fork to separate the grains, then add the rice to the wok or pan and stir-fry for 2 minutes until piping hot.

Add the sauce and basil leaves and stir-fry for a minute or two until the ingredients are evenly coated with the sauce, and the basil leaves have just started to wilt. Taste and season with salt and pepper if needed. Serve.

FAKEAWAYS

126

SLOW COOKER SPICED COCONUT BEEF STEW

🕐 **15 MINS**   🍲 **4 HRS 10 MINS–5 HRS 10 MINS**   ✕ **SERVES 4**

PER SERVING:
368 KCAL /13G CARBS

SPECIAL EQUIPMENT
3.5-litre slow cooker, food processor

low-calorie cooking spray
800g lean diced beef, all visible
   fat removed
¼ tsp ground cloves
1 star anise
¼ tsp ground cinnamon
½ tsp ground cardamom
400ml unsweetened coconut
   plant-based drink
2 tbsp tamarind paste
20g desiccated coconut
1 tsp white granulated
   sweetener or sugar
½ tsp salt

FOR THE SPICE PASTE
1 medium onion, peeled and cut
   into small chunks
4 garlic cloves, peeled
3cm (1¼in) piece of root ginger,
   peeled and cut into small
   chunks
1 medium red chilli, deseeded
finely grated zest and juice of
   ½ lime
2 tbsp lemongrass paste

TO ACCOMPANY
50g mini naan bread
   (+ 127 kcal per naan)

TIP:
You can use 2 fresh lemongrass
stalks. Trim away tough, woody
parts and blitz with the other
paste ingredients.

We've put together this warming Spiced Coconut Beef Stew with the flavours from a Southeast Asian Beef Rendang in mind. While traditional versions are usually dry with a thick, rich coating on the beef chunks, we've given you the option to ramp up the tastiness even more, by making our version with extra sauce. Every bite is bursting with aromatic ingredients, including coconut, tangy citrus and medium-hot spices. Before it all goes in the slow cooker, you'll brown the beef and cook up the homemade spice paste in a frying pan. It's well worth the small amount of extra washing-up – both steps do wonders for the flavours in this dish!

Weekly Indulgence

Put all the ingredients for the spice paste in a food processor and blitz to form a smooth paste. Set aside.

Spray a large frying pan with low-calorie cooking spray, place over a medium-high heat and, when hot, add the beef. Cook for 4–5 minutes until browned on all sides. Place the browned beef and any juices into the slow cooker.

Add the spice paste to the frying pan. Reduce the heat to medium and add the ground cloves, star anise, ground cinnamon, ground cardamom and stir. Cook for 4–5 minutes, stirring, until the spice paste is fragrant, then transfer to the slow cooker.

Add the coconut drink, tamarind paste, desiccated coconut, sweetener or sugar and the salt. Stir well. Cover with the lid and cook on high for 4–5 hours. When ready, the beef should be fall-apart tender and the sauce should be thickened. If you would like the stew to be thicker and drier, remove the lid and continue cooking for a little longer, until the sauce has reduced to the consistency you prefer.

Remove the star anise and serve.

FAKEAWAYS

GINGER MISO BEEF *with* NOODLES

🕐 **10 MINS***   🍲 **10 MINS**   ✕ **SERVES 2**

***PLUS 15 MINS MARINATING**

PER SERVING:
445 KCAL /50G CARBS

SPECIAL EQUIPMENT
Large, deep frying pan (about 28cm/11in) or non-stick wok

200g lean rump or sirloin steak, cut into strips
1 tsp toasted sesame oil
4 spring onions, trimmed and sliced
100g mangetout
250g pak choi, thinly slice the white stalks and roughly chop the green leaves
300g pack of straight-to-wok noodles

FOR THE MARINADE
2 tsp white miso paste
1 tbsp light soy sauce
5cm (2in) piece of root ginger, peeled and grated
2 garlic cloves, peeled and crushed
juice of 1 lime
½ tbsp runny honey

Who doesn't love a speedy stir-fry for dinner? Even allowing 15 minutes for the beef to marinate, this easy noodle dish is on the table in just over half an hour. The steak strips are coated in a salty-sweet mixture of soy sauce, honey and lime juice, with miso paste to bring a yummy umami flavour. Don't waste any marinade that isn't soaked up by the meat – pour it into the pan along with the beef, noodles and whichever vegetables you choose to use.

Weekly Indulgence

Mix the marinade ingredients together in a glass or plastic bowl and add the steak strips. Coat well, cover and leave for 15 minutes to marinate.

Place the wok or large frying pan over a high heat and add the sesame oil. Add the spring onions and stir-fry for a minute, then add the steak and any marinade remaining in the bowl and quickly stir-fry for 1–2 minutes. Add the mangetout and pak choi and cook for a further minute. You want to keep the vegetables crisp and bright.

Add the noodles and stir-fry for 3–4 minutes, until thoroughly heated through and well combined with the beef and vegetables. Serve.

TIP:
When slicing the steak into strips, cut across the grain. This will give you a much more tender piece of steak.

SPICY VEGETABLE FRIED RICE

🕐 **10 MINS**   🍲 **8 MINS**   ✕ **SERVES 2**

PER SERVING:
536 KCAL / 53G CARBS

SPECIAL EQUIPMENT
Wok or large frying pan

low-calorie cooking spray
4 spring onions, trimmed and sliced, white and green separated
100g frozen shelled edamame beans
2 carrots, peeled and cut into matchsticks
100g bean sprouts
50g sugar snap peas, sliced
1 x 250g pouch ready-cooked microwave basmati rice

FOR THE SAUCE
2 tsp toasted sesame oil
juice of 1 lime
1 tbsp dark soy sauce
1 tbsp sriracha (or other hot sauce)
2 tsp smooth peanut butter

TO SERVE
25g salted peanuts, roughly crushed
handful of fresh coriander, roughly chopped
1 red chilli, thinly sliced (remove seeds if you want it less fiery)

Did someone say vegan-friendly fakeaway night? This super quick fried rice is jam-packed with colourful vegetables and protein-rich beans, making it a feast in itself. To recreate tantalising, takeaway-style textures, cook the carrots and bean sprouts quickly so that they retain their crunch, and add a sprinkling of crushed peanuts for good measure. When you're making the sauce, don't skip the sesame oil – you don't want to miss out on those nutty, toasted flavours!

Special Occasion ——————————

In a small bowl, mix together the sauce ingredients until smooth and place to one side.

Spray the wok or frying pan with low-calorie cooking spray and place over a medium-high heat. When hot, add the white spring onions and edamame beans and stir-fry for 2–3 minutes. Add the carrots, bean sprouts and sugar snap peas and continue to cook for another 2 minutes, then add the rice to the pan (give the pouch a good squeeze before opening to separate the grains) and continue to stir-fry for a minute or two, until the rice and vegetables are well combined and piping hot.

Stir the sauce through the rice. The vegetables should be cooked through but still crunchy, and the rice should be piping hot.

Stir in the green spring onions, top with the crushed peanuts, coriander and chilli and serve.

TIP

We use a pouch of microwave rice for this, but you can use 250g leftover cooked rice, as long as it has been cooled quickly and stored correctly in a refrigerator (see page 13).

DAIRY
FREE

GLUTEN
FREE

USE GF
SOY SAUCE

CHINESE-STYLE STICKY PORK TRAYBAKE

🕐 **15 MINS**   🍲 **25 MINS**   ✕ **SERVES 4**

PER SERVING:
348 KCAL /44G CARBS

SPECIAL EQUIPMENT
Large baking tray with raised sides (about 38 x 26 x 2cm/ 15 x 10 x ¾in)

low-calorie cooking spray
4 thin pork loin steaks, visible fat removed (about 105g each)
1 medium red pepper, deseeded and thinly sliced
150g sugar snap peas
1 x 250g pouch ready-cooked microwave jasmine rice
150g pak choi, stalks and leaves cut into 3cm (1¼in) pieces
6 spring onions, trimmed and cut diagonally into 2–3cm (¾–1¼in) lengths
50g fresh bean sprouts
1 tsp sesame seeds
sea salt and freshly ground black pepper

FOR THE SAUCE
4 tbsp clear honey
2 tsp fine garlic granules
1 tbsp Chinese 5-spice powder
2 tsp dark soy sauce

TIP:
Jasmine rice in a pouch has already been cooked, so it should only be reheated once. To keep your family safe, this recipe should be eaten freshly made and not reheated.

Enjoying a Chinese-inspired meal at home doesn't have to mean reaching for the takeaway menu, and it definitely doesn't have to make a mess in your kitchen! To get your pork loin steaks succulent, aromatic and tasting like they've been delivered from a restaurant, you'll only need a baking tray, a mixing bowl, and a nifty combination of slimming-friendly ingredients for your sauce. Roast everything together, including the veg and fluffy jasmine rice, and you're onto an easy fakeaway-night winner.

Everyday Light ───────────

Preheat the oven to 200°C (fan 180°C/gas mark 4) and spray the large baking tray with a little low-calorie cooking spray.

Place the sauce ingredients in a small bowl and mix well. Set aside.

Place the pork steaks on the baking tray and arrange the red pepper and sugar snap peas in between and around them. Drizzle half the sauce over the pork steaks and vegetables, then cook in the oven for 15 minutes.

Tip the jasmine rice from its pouch into a bowl and break it up with a fork to separate the grains.

Remove the tray from the oven and scatter the rice evenly around the pork steaks, on top of the peppers and sugar snap peas. Place the pak choi, spring onions and bean sprouts around the pork steaks, on top of the vegetables and rice. Drizzle the remaining sauce over the pork, vegetables and rice and sprinkle over the sesame seeds.

Return to the oven for 10 minutes, turning the vegetables and rice halfway through. The pork steaks should be cooked thoroughly, show no sign of pinkness, and their juices should run clear. The vegetables should be tender, retaining a little crispness and their fresh green colour. The rice should be piping hot. Season to taste with salt and pepper and serve.

SLOW COOKER SWEET *and* SOUR PORK NOODLES

🕐 **15 MINS**　　🍲 **5 HRS**　　✕ **SERVES 4**

PER SERVING:
506 KCAL /65G CARBS

SPECIAL EQUIPMENT
3.5-litre slow cooker

low-calorie cooking spray
600g diced pork, any visible fat removed
1 medium red pepper, deseeded and sliced
1 medium green pepper, deseeded and sliced
1 medium red onion, peeled and roughly chopped
160g fresh pineapple, sliced into chunks
4 garlic cloves, peeled and crushed
200ml boiling water
1 chicken stock cube
3 tbsp soy sauce
2 tbsp honey
2 tbsp white granulated sweetener
1 tbsp rice vinegar
1 tbsp tomato puree
1 tsp ground ginger
1 tsp sriracha sauce
1 tsp garlic granules
2 tbsp cornflour, mixed to a slurry with 2 tbsp water
130g dried egg noodles
100g sugar snap peas, halved vertically
sea salt and freshly ground black pepper
2 spring onions, trimmed and thinly sliced, to serve

Your local takeaway can't compete with these Sweet and Sour Pork Noodles! Far better for you and your budget than restaurant versions, we've used slow-cooked pork pieces, juicy pineapple and fiery sriracha to recreate trademark sweet and sour flavours. Don't be put off by the length of our ingredients list – your slow cooker will do the hard work for you, by slowly simmering herbs, spices and store-cupboard staples into a gloriously sticky homemade sauce. Stir the noodles in when you're back from work and your fakeaway feast will be ready in no time.

Special Occasion

Spray a pan with low-calorie cooking spray and place over a medium heat. Add the pork and fry for 3–4 minutes, until browned on all sides.

Put the browned pork in the slow cooker pot, along with the peppers, onion, pineapple and garlic.

In a jug or bowl, combine the water, stock cube, soy sauce, honey, sweetener, rice vinegar, tomato puree, ginger, sriracha and garlic granules. Mix, then pour over the pork and vegetables in the slow cooker. Stir in the cornflour slurry and mix well. Cover with the lid and cook on low for 4½ hours.

Add the egg noodles and submerge into the veg and pork, re-cover and cook for 15 minutes. Stir and add the sugar snap peas, re-cover and cook for a final 15 minutes. Season to taste with salt and pepper. Serve topped with the spring onions.

IF YOU DON'T HAVE A SLOW COOKER
Alternatively, cook this in the oven. Preheat the oven to 180°C (fan 160°C/gas mark 4) and follow the steps above, adding everything to a casserole dish. Cover and cook for 1 hour. Add the noodles and sugar snap peas and cook for a further 15–20 minutes. The vegetables and noodles should be soft, and the pork cooked through.

TIP:
You can swap the fresh pineapple for tinned, if you prefer.

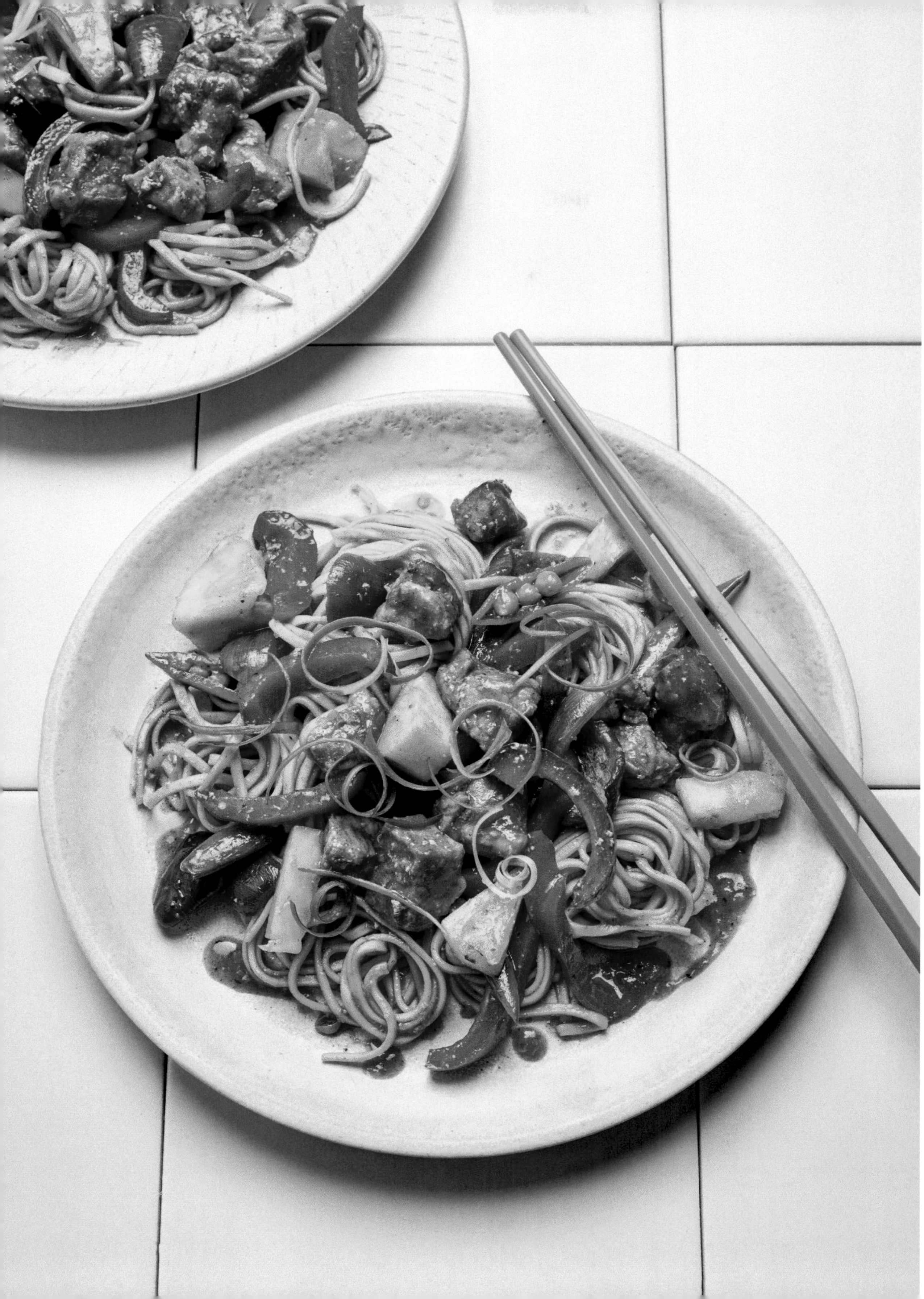

SLOW COOKER STICKY BBQ RIBS

🕐 **10 MINS**　　🍲 **2 HRS 45 MINS–3 HRS 15 MINS**　　✕ **MAKES 8**

PER RIB:
236 KCAL /12G CARBS

SPECIAL EQUIPMENT
3.5-litre slow cooker,
ovenproof dish or roasting tin
(about 20 x 30cm/8 x 12in)

8 pork ribs (about 700g total)
200ml (400ml for oven method)
  chicken stock (1 chicken stock
  cube dissolved in 200/400ml
  boiling water)

FOR THE DRY RUB
2 tsp smoked paprika
2 tsp garlic powder
1 tsp onion powder
¼ tsp cayenne pepper
½ tsp salt
½ tsp freshly ground black
  pepper

FOR THE BBQ SAUCE
4 tbsp tomato ketchup
3 tbsp runny honey
2 tbsp Worcestershire sauce or
  Henderson's relish
2 tbsp cider vinegar
1 tbsp dark soy sauce
2 tsp smoked paprika
2 tsp garlic powder
1 tsp onion powder
½ tsp mustard powder
½ tsp salt
½ tsp ground black pepper

TO ACCOMPANY *(optional)*
75g mixed salad (+ 15 kcal per
  125g cooked serving)

A proper tasty starter, side or snack, these slow-cooked Sticky BBQ Ribs are a slimming-friendly dream! Coated in a delightfully sticky, smoky-sweet sauce, they're flavourful, fall-off-the-bone tender and far lighter than restaurant versions. We've counted out the calories per rib, so you can easily keep track of where you're up to. Try them on their own, or pair them with your favourite accompaniments from a classic BBQ spread (we'd go for coleslaw and creamy potato salad!).

Weekly Indulgence ───────────

Place the smoked paprika, garlic powder, onion powder, cayenne pepper, salt and black pepper in a small bowl and mix. Put the ribs on a plate and sprinkle over the dry rub, then rub the mix into the ribs to coat all over.

Place the coated ribs in the slow cooker and pour in the stock. Cover with the lid and cook on high for 2½–3 hours. The ribs should be cooked, with no pinkness inside, and the pork should be fall-apart tender.

Place all the sauce ingredients in a small saucepan and place over a medium heat. Simmer gently for about 5 minutes, until thick and sticky. Set aside.

When the ribs are cooked, remove them from the stock. Place the drained ribs in a single layer in an ovenproof dish or roasting tin. Preheat the grill on the high setting. Pour the BBQ sauce over the drained ribs, turning to coat on all sides. Place under the hot grill for 5–10 minutes, turning once, until the ribs are browning around the edges and sticky. Keep a close eye on the ribs while grilling as they can burn easily. Serve.

IF YOU DON'T HAVE A SLOW COOKER
To cook the ribs in the oven, preheat the oven to 170°C (fan 150°C/gas mark 3) and make the dry rub as above. Place the coated ribs in a single layer in an ovenproof dish or roasting tin, about 20 x 30cm (8 x 12in). Pour over 400ml chicken stock and cover tightly with foil. Bake in the oven for 2 hours until the ribs are cooked, with no pinkness inside and the pork is fall-apart tender, then remove from the stock, pour over the sauce and grill (see above).

FAKEAWAYS

SLOW COOKER CIDER PULLED PORK

🕐 **20 MINS**   🍲 **6 HRS**   ✕ **SERVES 10**

PER SERVING:
150 KCAL /4.8G CARBS

SPECIAL EQUIPMENT
3.5-litre slow cooker

1kg pork shoulder joint, all
   visible fat removed
500ml apple cider
200ml apple juice

FOR THE RUB
2 tsp white granulated
   sweetener
1 tsp smoked paprika
1 tsp mild chilli powder
1 tsp garlic powder
1 tsp mustard powder
¼ tsp ground cinnamon
¼ tsp ground ginger
½ tsp salt
½ tsp freshly ground black
   pepper

FOR THE SAUCE
2 tbsp tomato puree
2 tsp white granulated
   sweetener

TO ACCOMPANY *(optional)*
60g wholemeal bread roll
   (+ 146 kcal per roll)

You can't go wrong when you put pork and apple together! For this crowd-pleasing pulled pork recipe, we've poured a mixture of cider and apple juice over a spice-rubbed pork shoulder joint, then left the slow cooker to work its magic. It's all about minimum effort and maximum flavour with this one! Once the pork is fall-off-the-fork tender, it's ready to be shredded and coated in the gorgeous sauce made from the cooking juices. There are almost too many ways to enjoy the finished result – try pulled pork sliders, use it as a baked potato topping or spoon it over rice.

Everyday Light ───────────────────

Combine the rub ingredients in a small bowl, then rub the mix into the pork, covering the whole surface. Place the pork into the bottom of the slow cooker pot.

Put the cider and apple juice in a jug then pour into the slow cooker. Cover with the lid and cook on high for 6 hours.

Remove the liquid from the slow cooker and put to one side. We found a ladle helpful, but you could use a large spoon or carefully pour the liquid out of the slow cooker pot.

Shred the pork in the slow cooker using two forks, until any large bits are broken up. Pour 150ml of the cooking liquid into a heatproof jug or bowl, add the tomato puree and sweetener and stir until combined. Discard any remaining liquid. Pour the sauce over the shredded pork and stir to coat. Serve with your choice of accompaniment.

TIP:
Try not to open your slow cooker while cooking, as this will reduce the temperature .

VEGGIE
USE PLANT-BASED MINCE AND VEGGIE STOCK CUBE

VEGAN
USE PLANT-BASED MINCE, STOCK AND CHEESE

DAIRY FREE
USE DF CHEESE

GLUTEN FREE
USE GF STOCK CUBE AND TORTILLA CHIPS

CHILLI TORTILLA PIE

🕐 **15 MINS** 🍲 **35 MINS** ✕ **SERVES 4**

PER SERVING:
547 KCAL /50G CARBS

SPECIAL EQUIPMENT
28cm (11in) shallow casserole dish with a tight-fitting lid

low-calorie cooking spray
500g 5%-fat minced beef
1 onion, peeled and diced
2 peppers (mixed colours), deseeded and diced
4 garlic cloves, peeled and crushed
1 tbsp mild chilli powder
1 tsp ground cumin
1 x 400g tin chopped tomatoes
300ml beef stock (1 beef stock cube dissolved in 300ml boiling water)
1 x 250g pouch ready-cooked microwave basmati rice
1 x 400g tin black beans in water, drained and rinsed
juice of 1 lime
handful of fresh coriander, roughly chopped
sea salt and freshly ground black pepper

FOR THE TOPPING
40g bag tortilla chips
80g reduced-fat mature Cheddar, finely grated
1 red chilli, thinly sliced (*optional*)

TIP:
This is quite a mild dish, but you can increase the spiciness by using hot chilli powder and garnishing it with more fresh sliced chillies. Try using hot and spicy flavoured tortilla chips for even more of a kick

Who's up for chilli tonight? Forget faffing around making the chilli, rice and nachos separately – you can make everything in one casserole dish! This Chilli Tortilla Pie saves a whole load of washing up, and it's fun to make too. We use mild chilli powder to give the dish a subtle kick, so this recipe is nice and family friendly. The 'pie' topping is made with tortilla chips, covered in cheese and popped under a hot grill until gooey and gloriouser.

Special Occasion —————————————

Spray the casserole dish with low-calorie cooking spray and place over a medium-high heat. Add the minced beef and cook for 5 minutes, breaking it up with a wooden spoon, until browned, then add the onion, peppers and garlic and cook for a further 5 minutes.

Add the chilli powder and cumin, then stir in the chopped tomatoes and stock. Bring to the boil then reduce the heat to a simmer, cover and cook for 15 minutes.

Give the rice pouch a good squeeze before opening, to separate the grains, then stir into the chilli, along with the beans and lime juice. Bring back to a simmer and cook, uncovered, for 5 minutes, until the rice and beans are thoroughly heated through.

Preheat the grill to medium setting.

Stir in the coriander (reserving some for garnish), taste and season with salt and pepper if required.

Turn off the heat. Scatter the tortilla chips evenly over the top and sprinkle with the grated cheese. Place under the grill for a few minutes, until the cheese is melted and the tortilla chips are golden brown and crispy. Sprinkle over the remaining coriander and the sliced chilli (if using). Serve.

FAKEAWAYS

FREEZE ME

OMIT GRATED CHEESE AND BURGER SAUCE

BATCH COOK

DAIRY FREE

USE DF CHEESE

GLUTEN FREE

USE GF STOCK CUBE AND HENDERSON'S RELISH

CHEESEBURGER DIRTY RICE

🕐 **15 MINS**   🍲 **15 MINS**   ✕ **SERVES 4**

PER SERVING:
390 KCAL /43G CARBS

low-calorie cooking spray
2 bacon medallions, diced
1 medium red onion, peeled and diced
3 garlic cloves, peeled and crushed
250g 5%-fat minced beef
1 tsp smoked paprika
½ tsp ground cumin
½ tsp onion granules
½ tsp garlic granules
1 beef stock cube, crumbled
150ml boiling water
1 tbsp tomato puree
1 tbsp Henderson's relish or Worcestershire sauce
2 x 250g pouches ready-cooked microwave basmati rice
60g pickled gherkins, roughly chopped
6 cherry tomatoes, diced
sea salt and freshly ground black pepper
20g reduced-fat mature Cheddar cheese, grated, to serve

FOR THE BURGER SAUCE
3 tbsp reduced-fat mayonnaise
½ tsp reduced sugar and salt tomato ketchup
2 tsp gherkin pickling vinegar or rice vinegar
¼ tsp smoked paprika

A must-try for your next fakeaway night, we've mixed all the best bits of a cheeseburger into some fluffy basmati rice for this easy dinner. We're talking seasoned mince, bacon, gherkins, tomatoes, cheese and our unmissable homemade burger sauce. Quick and easy to throw together, this one deserves a spot on your meal plan, especially if you've tried and loved our Dirty Rice or Cajun-style

Everyday Light ───────────────

Spray a large frying pan with low-calorie cooking spray and place over a medium heat. Add the bacon, onion and garlic and cook for 4 minutes, until just softening and the bacon is starting to turn brown, then add the minced beef and continue to cook for 3–4 minutes until browned all over, breaking it up with a wooden spoon. Add the paprika, cumin, onion granules and garlic granules and fry for another minute. Add the beef stock cube to the water, along with the tomato puree and Henderson's relish or Worcestershire sauce, stir to combine and pour into the pan. Simmer gently for 5 minutes until thickened and rich.

Give the pouches of rice a good squeeze to break up any clumps, then pop the rice into the pan and stir well. When the rice is well coated and piping hot, stir in the gherkins and cherry tomatoes. Season with salt and pepper.

To make the burger sauce, combine the mayonnaise, tomato ketchup, vinegar and paprika in a small bowl.

Serve the rice with a sprinkle of grated cheese and a drizzle of the burger sauce.

TOMATO *and* PARMESAN RISOTTO

🕐 **5 MINS**   🍲 **35 MINS**   ✕ **SERVES 4**

PER SERVING:
426 KCAL / 71G CARBS

low-calorie cooking spray
1 onion, peeled and finely
   chopped
4 garlic cloves, peeled and
   crushed
300g arborio rice
juice of ½ lemon
500g passata
1 litre vegetable stock (1
   vegetable stock cube dissolved
   in 1 litre of boiling water)
75g reduced-fat cream cheese
50g Parmesan, grated
handful of basil leaves,
   chopped (reserve a few whole
   leaves for garnish)
sea salt and freshly ground
   black pepper

Sometimes, the simplest recipes are the very best. This creamy one-pot risotto is so impressive, you'd never guess it's made with a short list of tasty, budget-friendly ingredients. Starting with a rich base of garlicky, pan-fried onions and passata, you gradually add stock until your arborio rice has the perfect tender texture. With a gentle helping of cream cheese, salty Parmesan and fresh basil, this velvety risotto is too good to only enjoy once (luckily, it freezes like a dream!).

Weekly Indulgence

Spray a large saucepan with low-calorie cooking spray and place over a medium heat. Add the onion and garlic and cook for about 5 minutes, until soft and golden, then add the rice and cook for another minute or two, stirring well to coat the rice in the garlicky flavours. Add the lemon juice and passata and bring to the boil, stirring constantly.

Reduce the heat so the risotto is gently bubbling, and keep stirring for about 5 minutes until the passata is almost all absorbed.

Add a ladleful of the hot stock and stir until completely absorbed. Continue to add the stock, a ladleful at a time, stirring until it is all absorbed. This should take 20–25 minutes in total. The risotto should be creamy and the rice tender but still holding its shape.

Stir in the cream cheese, Parmesan and chopped basil.

Taste and season with salt and pepper, if required. Serve, garnished with whole basil leaves.

The dish will keep in the fridge for up to 3 days.

TIP:

If you've frozen the risotto, when reheating after defrosting, you may need to add a splash of water if it has dried out a little.

VEGGIE
USE VEGGIE ITALIAN HARD CHEESE

VEGAN
USE DF HARD CHEESE AND CREAM CHEESE

FREEZE ME

BATCH COOK

DAIRY FREE
USE PLANT-BASED HARD CHEESE AND CREAM CHEESE

GLUTEN FREE
USE GF STOCK CUBE

FAKEAWAYS

VEGGIE

USE VEGGIE FETA

VEGAN

USE VEGAN FETA

DAIRY FREE

USE DF FETA

GLUTEN FREE

USE GF STOCK CUBES

SLOW COOKER SWEET POTATO *and* FETA RISOTTO

🕐 **10 MINS**　　🍲 **1½–2 HRS**　　✕ **SERVES 4**

PER SERVING:
293 KCAL /52G CARBS

SPECIAL EQUIPMENT
3.5-litre slow cooker

2 large shallots, peeled and
　very finely chopped
200g sweet potato, peeled
　and cut into 1cm (½in) dice
4 garlic cloves, crushed
1 tsp Italian mixed herbs
900ml hot vegetable stock
　(2 vegetable stock cubes
　dissolved in 900ml boiling
　water)
juice of 1 lemon
200g risotto rice
100g reduced-fat feta,
　crumbled
sea salt and freshly ground
　black pepper

Risotto is one of those dishes that's delicious to eat, but a chore to cook. Not with this recipe up your sleeve! There's no standing around and stirring when you let your slow cooker do all the hard work for you. Once you've loaded in the ingredients, you'll only need to stir once or twice during the 90 minutes it takes to cook. Don't worry, even though it's low on effort, you still end up with big flavours! It turns out creamy and filling, with sweetness from the potatoes that's perfectly balanced by the salty, tangy feta cheese.

Everyday Light ——————————

Put all the ingredients, except the feta, into the slow cooker. Set to high, cover with the lid and cook for 50 minutes. Stir and cook, re-covered, for a further 40–50 minutes.

When cooked, the rice should be tender and creamy, but still holding its shape. Stir in half the crumbled feta, taste and season with salt and pepper if required. Serve topped with the remaining feta.

TIPS:

If the stock is hot when adding it to the slow cooker pot, it will give a more accurate cooking time.

If you have time, sauté the shallots in a little low-calorie cooking spray before adding them to the pot. This will improve the texture and flavour of the dish.

FAKEAWAYS

USE GF
STOCK CUBE
AND PASTA

HARISSA CHICKEN MAC 'N' CHEESE

🕐 **10 MINS**   🍲 **40 MINS**   ✕ **SERVES 4**

PER SERVING:
450 KCAL /45G CARBS

SPECIAL EQUIPMENT
Deep casserole dish with tight-fitting lid (about 24cm/9¾in), suitable for hob and under grill

low-calorie cooking spray
1 medium onion, peeled and
  finely chopped
4 garlic cloves, peeled and
  crushed
300g diced chicken breast
3 tbsp harissa paste (we use
  one with a medium heat)
300ml low-salt chicken stock
  (1 low-salt chicken stock cube
  dissolved in 300ml boiling
  water)
300ml skimmed milk
200g dried macaroni
80g tenderstem broccoli, cut in
  half lengthways
175g reduced-fat mature
  Cheddar spreadable cheese
15g Parmesan, finely grated
freshly ground black pepper

FOR THE TOP
15g Parmesan, finely grated
1 tbsp hot pepper sauce

TIP:
We use a reduced-fat mature Cheddar spreadable cheese such as Seriously Spreadable Lighter. It has a strong cheesy flavour and consistency that melts to form the cheese sauce in this recipe. Cream cheese would not be suitable in this recipe.

We've given macaroni cheese a North African-inspired twist to create this unexpected flavour combination! Harissa is a tangy paste of chilli, garlic and other spices that comes in a variety of different heat options. We've used medium-spicy harissa to coat the tender chicken chunks in this recipe. We love that you don't need to mess around making a flour-based cheese sauce in a separate pot – simply stir in some spreadable cheese, sprinkle with Parmesan, grill until golden and you're ready to serve.

Weekly Indulgence

Spray the deep casserole dish with low-calorie cooking spray and place over a medium heat. Add the onion and cook for 10 minutes, until soft and golden, then add the garlic, chicken and harissa paste and stir well. Cook for 10 minutes, until the chicken is cooked and shows no sign of pinkness inside.

Add the stock, milk and macaroni and stir well to ensure the macaroni isn't sticking together. Bring to the boil, cover with a tight-fitting lid and lower the heat. Simmer gently for 10 minutes, stirring occasionally, or until the pasta is tender and the sauce has thickened slightly.

Add the broccoli, cover and simmer for 4–5 minutes, or until the broccoli is tender, but still retains its bright green colour.

Stir in the spreadable cheese and 15g Parmesan, until well combined and the pasta is coated with cheese sauce.

Season to taste with pepper. Preheat the grill on a medium setting.

Sprinkle over the remaining grated Parmesan and place under the preheated grill for about 5 minutes, or until bubbling and golden on top. Drizzle over the hot pepper sauce and serve.

The dish will keep in the fridge for up to 3 days.

FAKEAWAYS

FREEZE ME

BATCH COOK

DAIRY FREE

USE DF CREAM CHEESE AND PARMESAN

GLUTEN FREE

USE GF STOCK CUBE AND PASTA

CREAMY TOMATO, BACON *and* SPINACH PASTA

🕐 **10 MINS**　　🍲 **45 MINS**　　✕ **SERVES 4**

PER SERVING:
489 KCAL / 66G CARBS

SPECIAL EQUIPMENT
Deep casserole dish with tight-fitting lid (about 24cm/9¾in), suitable for oven and hob

low-calorie cooking spray
1 medium onion, peeled and finely chopped
2 garlic cloves, peeled and crushed
8 smoked bacon medallions, cut into 1–2cm (½–¾in) dice
500g passata
1 tbsp tomato puree
½ tsp mild chilli powder
1 tsp white granulated sweetener or granulated sugar
600ml low-salt vegetable or chicken stock (1 low-salt vegetable or chicken stock cube dissolved in 600ml boiling water)
300g dried pasta shapes (we used penne)
75g reduced-fat cream cheese
80g baby spinach leaves
freshly ground black pepper
15g Parmesan, finely grated

TIPS:

We used penne, but use a pasta shape of your choice.

Make sure to use white granulated sweetener that has a similar weight, texture and sweetness as sugar, not the powdered type.

In the middle of the week you need something easy and tasty, that's on the table in less than an hour. This Creamy Tomato, Bacon and Spinach Pasta ticks every box, filling your plate with homely, hearty flavours. To keep the calories down, we've melted reduced-fat cream cheese into the rich, tomatoey sauce, making it velvety without the need for heavy cream. The hint of chilli powder gives this dish a lovely warming taste, but feel free to add more to ramp up the spiciness.

Weekly Indulgence

Spray the deep casserole dish with low-calorie cooking spray and place over a medium heat. Add the onion and cook for 10 minutes, until soft and golden, then add the garlic and cook for a further 2 minutes. Add the bacon and cook for 4–5 minutes, until cooked through.

Add the passata, tomato puree, chilli powder, sweetener or sugar and stir well. Bring to the boil, cover with a tight-fitting lid and lower the heat. Simmer gently for 15 minutes.

Add the stock and stir, then add the pasta, stirring well to ensure the pasta shapes aren't sticking together and bring to the boil. Lower the heat to medium, cover and simmer for 10 minutes, stirring occasionally, until the pasta is tender, and the sauce has thickened.

Remove from the heat, add the cream cheese and stir until completely blended. Add the spinach and stir in. Return to the heat, cover and simmer for 2–3 minutes, until the spinach has just wilted and the pasta is piping hot. Season to taste with pepper, sprinkle with the Parmesan and serve.

The dish will keep in the fridge for up to 3 days.

FAKEAWAYS

CHEESY BEEF RAGU

🕐 **15 MINS**   🍲 **50 MINS**   ✕ **SERVES 4**

PER SERVING:
372 KCAL /35G CARBS

SPECIAL EQUIPMENT
Shallow casserole dish with tight-fitting lid (about 28cm/11in), suitable for oven and hob

low-calorie cooking spray
1 medium onion, peeled and diced
4 garlic cloves, peeled and crushed
1 medium red pepper, deseeded and finely diced
500g 5%-fat minced beef
1 x 400g tin chopped tomatoes
1 medium carrot, peeled and finely grated
2 red wine stock pots
1 beef stock cube, crumbled
2 tbsp Worcestershire sauce or Henderson's relish
2 tbsp tomato puree
large handful of fresh basil leaves, roughly torn
40g baby spinach leaves
250g ready-prepared gnocchi
40g reduced-fat mature Cheddar, finely grated
freshly ground black pepper

TO ACCOMPANY
75g mixed salad
(+ 15 kcal per serving)

TIP:

If you've frozen the dish, when reheating after defrosting, you may need to add a splash of water if it has dried out a little.

If you're looking out for an Italian-inspired winter warmer, you're on the right page. Our savoury and rich beef ragu is topped with a golden layer of melted reduced-fat Cheddar cheese, and dumpling-like gnocchi soak up the flavours like a dream. We use red wine stock pots to keep the calories down, but if you're in the mood for a more luxurious meal, there's nothing to stop you using a glass of the real stuff! It's sure to become a firm favourite for chillier evenings.

Everyday Light

Spray the large, shallow casserole dish with low-calorie cooking spray and place over a medium heat. Add the onion, garlic and red pepper and cook for 10 minutes until soft, then add the minced beef and cook for 4–5 minutes until browned, breaking it up with a wooden spoon. Add the chopped tomatoes, carrot, red wine stock pots, crumbled beef stock cube (no need to dissolve it in water), Worcestershire sauce or Henderson's relish and tomato puree. Stir well, cover with a tight-fitting lid and simmer gently for 30 minutes, stirring occasionally, until the mixture is thick and rich.

Stir in the basil and spinach leaves until just wilted but still bright green, and season with pepper, then stir in the gnocchi, sprinkle over the grated Cheddar and simmer gently for a couple of minutes (lid off), to heat up the gnocchi and melt the cheese. Serve with a mixed salad.

We've suggested this accompaniment to ensure this is a true, all-in-one recipe. You can enjoy this dish with any accompaniment you like, but don't forget to adjust the calories accordingly.

The ragu will keep in the fridge for up to 3 days.

FAKEAWAYS

SLOW COOKER CREAMY CHICKEN *and* SWEETCORN PASTA

🕐 **5 MINS**   🍲 **3 HRS 40 MINS–6 HRS 40 MINS**   ✕ **SERVES 4**

PER SERVING:
499 KCAL /57G CARBS

SPECIAL EQUIPMENT
3.5-litre slow cooker

400g diced chicken breast
1 onion, peeled and finely chopped
3 garlic cloves, peeled and crushed
150g frozen or tinned, drained sweetcorn
1 tsp dried chilli flakes
800ml chicken stock (1 chicken stock cube dissolved in 800ml boiling water)
2 tbsp cornflour, mixed to a slurry with 2 tbsp water
75g reduced-fat cream cheese
50g sun-dried tomatoes, finely chopped
200g small dried pasta shapes (we used penne)
80g reduced-fat Cheddar, grated
freshly ground black pepper

This slow-cooked pasta dish is a game-changer! We're talking penne pasta pieces in an oh-so-cheesy homemade sauce with tender chicken chunks, crunchy sweetcorn and juicy sun-dried tomatoes, all ready to serve by the time you walk through the door after work. You can leave it to bubble for 3 hours on high, or 5–6 on low, depending on your schedule. Either way, the sauce will be thick and creamy, ready to sprinkle with as much reduced-fat grated Cheddar as you'd like. Sit back, relax and tuck in...with or without a side of garlic bread!

Weekly Indulgence

Put the diced chicken, onion, garlic, sweetcorn and chilli flakes in the slow cooker pot. Stir in the stock and cornflour slurry. Cover with the lid and cook on high for 3 hours, or 5–6 hours on low.

Stir in the cream cheese, sun-dried tomatoes and pasta, re-cover with the lid and cook for a further 40 minutes, stirring halfway through (if cooking on low setting, increase to high). There will be a lot of sauce, but this will thicken as the pasta cooks and absorbs the liquid.

Stir in the grated Cheddar, season with freshly ground pepper, to taste, and serve.

TIP:
If you've frozen it, you may need to add a splash of water when reheating as it can dry out in the freezer.

FAKEAWAYS

CHICKEN, BACON *and* LEEK MACARONI

🕐 **10 MINS**   🍲 **35 MINS**   ✕ **SERVES 4**

PER SERVING:
496 KCAL /47G CARBS

SPECIAL EQUIPMENT
Deep casserole dish with tight-fitting lid (about 24cm/9in), suitable for hob and under grill

low-calorie cooking spray
½ medium onion, peeled and finely chopped
1 large leek, trimmed and chopped
4 garlic cloves, peeled and crushed
300g diced chicken breast
4 smoked bacon medallions, diced
300ml chicken stock (1 chicken stock cube dissolved in 300ml boiling water)
300ml skimmed milk
200g dried macaroni
1 tsp chopped fresh thyme leaves
2 tsp Dijon mustard
175g reduced-fat mature Cheddar spreadable cheese
15g Parmesan, finely grated
freshly ground black pepper

FOR THE TOP
15g panko breadcrumbs
15g Parmesan, finely grated
1 tbsp chopped curly parsley

TIPS:
You could use ½ teaspoon dried thyme instead of the fresh thyme.

This freezes well. When reheating after defrosting, you may need to add a splash of water.

You might not expect to be able to make macaroni cheese all in one pot, but with this simple (and delicious) recipe you can! We've loaded our extra-cheesy pasta dish with chicken and bacon, to make it feel especially decadent. You'd never be able to tell from the taste that we've used reduced-fat spreadable cheese to make the creamy, slimming-friendly sauce. As a final step, don't skip toasting the breadcrumb topping under the grill – it adds the perfect golden crunch.

Weekly Indulgence

Spray the deep casserole dish with low-calorie cooking spray and place over a medium heat. Add the onion and leek and cook for 10 minutes, until soft and golden, then add the garlic, chicken and bacon and stir well. Cook for 10 minutes, until the chicken is cooked and shows no sign of pinkness inside.

Add the stock, milk, macaroni, thyme and mustard and stir well to ensure the macaroni isn't sticking together.

Bring to the boil, cover with a tight-fitting lid and lower the heat. Simmer gently for 10 minutes, stirring occasionally, or until the pasta is tender and the sauce has thickened slightly.

Stir in the spreadable cheese and 15g Parmesan until well combined and the pasta is coated with cheese sauce. Season to taste with freshly ground black pepper. Preheat the grill on a medium setting.

In a small bowl, mix the breadcrumbs and Parmesan for the top and sprinkle it over the macaroni. Place under the preheated grill for about 5 minutes or until bubbling and the top is golden and crunchy. Sprinkle with chopped parsley and serve.

The dish will keep in the fridge for 1–2 days.

FAKEAWAYS

CHEESY SALMON *and* LEEK ORZOTTO

🕐 **15 MINS**   🍲 **35 MINS**   ✕ **SERVES 4**

PER SERVING:
460 KCAL /42G CARBS

SPECIAL EQUIPMENT
Large, shallow casserole dish, suitable for hob (about 28cm/11in), or large, deep frying pan

low-calorie cooking spray
1 medium onion, peeled and chopped
2 medium leeks, trimmed and chopped (about 250g total)
2 tsp garlic granules
600ml fish or chicken stock (1 fish or chicken stock cube dissolved in 600ml boiling water)
200g dried orzo
150g baby corn, sliced into 2–3cm (¾–1¼in) chunks
2 skinless, boneless salmon fillets (about 125g each), cut into 4cm (1½in) chunks
80g sugar snap peas
juice of 1 lemon
handful of fresh coriander leaves, chopped
120g reduced-fat mature Cheddar, finely grated
sea salt and freshly ground black pepper

With fresh, lemony flavours and crisp, crunchy vegetables, there's something summery about this Cheesy Salmon and Leek Orzotto. We've made two salmon fillets stretch so much further by bulking out the recipe with orzo pasta and plenty of veggies. Simmered on the hob until the creamy sauce has a similar texture to risotto, this is an easy-peasy fish dish that the whole family will look forward to!

Weekly Indulgence

Spray the large, shallow casserole dish or large, deep frying pan with low-calorie cooking spray and place over a medium heat.

Add the onion and leeks and cook for about 10 minutes, or until soft and golden.

Add the garlic granules and stock, stir, then bring to the boil. Add the orzo and baby corn and stir well, making sure that the orzo is covered by the liquid. Reduce the heat to a simmer, cover and cook gently for 10 minutes, stirring frequently so that the orzo doesn't stick to the pan.

Add the salmon chunks and sugar snap peas, cover and cook gently for a further 10–15 minutes, stirring occasionally and taking care not to break up the salmon too much.

The orzo and salmon should be cooked, the vegetables should be tender but retaining a little crispness, and most of the liquid absorbed. Uncover and stir in the lemon juice and coriander. If there is excess liquid, continue to cook, uncovered, for a few more minutes. The mixture should resemble a creamy risotto.

Stir in the grated cheese until melted. Season with salt and pepper to taste and serve.

The dish will keep in the fridge for up to 2 days.

TIP:
If you prefer, you can swap sugar snap peas for mangetout or frozen peas.

FAKEAWAYS

CREAMY CHICKEN LASAGNE

🕐 **15 MINS**   🍲 **30 MINS**   ✕ **SERVES 4**

PER SERVING:
481 KCAL /41G CARBS

SPECIAL EQUIPMENT
28cm (11in) shallow casserole dish or deep frying pan, suitable for hob and oven

low-calorie cooking spray
400g chicken breast, cut into small strips
1 onion, peeled and finely diced
100g button mushrooms, thinly sliced
2 garlic cloves, peeled and crushed
500ml chicken stock (1 chicken stock cube dissolved in 500ml boiling water)
125g tinned sweetcorn, drained
1 tbsp cornflour, mixed to a slurry with 1 tbsp water
100g reduced-fat cream cheese
good handful of fresh basil leaves, roughly torn, plus a few extra to serve (optional)
6 dried lasagne sheets
100g reduced-fat mature Cheddar, finely grated
125g reduced-fat mozzarella
freshly ground black pepper

TO ACCOMPANY (optional)
75g mixed salad (+ 15 kcal per serving)

TIP:
Use 'light' or 'medium-fat' cream cheese for this recipe. They are more stable in the oven. Using a 'lightest' cream cheese, could cause the sauce to split in the oven.

This recipe is a delicious way to satisfy your lasagne cravings, without the usual pile of washing-up that follows! The big difference here is that you don't need to worry about building things up layer by layer. Chop your ingredients nice and small and it'll be ten times easier to slide your lasagne sheets into the dish or pan. Our non-traditional filling of chicken, mushrooms and sweetcorn pairs like a dream with our oh-so-cheesy white sauce.

Weekly Indulgence

Preheat the oven to 200°C (fan 180°C/gas mark 6).

Spray the shallow casserole dish or deep frying pan with low-calorie cooking spray and place over a medium heat.

Add the chicken strips and onion and fry for 5 minutes, until the chicken is sealed and the onions are starting to soften, then add the mushrooms and garlic and cook for 2–3 minutes until soft. Add the stock and sweetcorn and bring to the boil, then reduce the heat to a simmer. Stir in the cornflour slurry and continue stirring until the sauce thickens. Stir in the cream cheese until well combined and you have a creamy sauce that coats the back of your spoon.

Add the basil leaves and season with black pepper. Remove from the heat and place the pan on a stable surface.

Take 3 of the lasagne sheets and break each one into 4. You should have 12 pieces. Slide each piece into the pan at a 45-degree angle, then take a long-handled spoon and bury each piece deep into the sauce. Make sure they are evenly spaced and try not to overlap them too much. Take the remaining 3 lasagne sheets and break them in half, widthways, so you have 6 rough squares. Place one in the centre of the pan, flat on top of the sauce. Arrange the other 5 around the outside. Take your spoon and gently press each down, so they are just lightly covered by the sauce.

Sprinkle over the grated Cheddar, then tear the mozzarella into small pieces and dot evenly over the top. Bake in the oven and cook for 30 minutes, until the top is golden. Serve garnished with some fresh basil leaves, if you wish.

The lasagne will keep in the fridge for up to 3 days.

FAKEAWAYS

BAKES and ROASTS

SPANISH-STYLE CHICKEN TRAYBAKE

🕐 **15 MINS*** 🍲 **55 MINS** ✕ **SERVES 4**

*PLUS 30 MINS MARINATING

PER SERVING:
355 KCAL /26G CARBS

SPECIAL EQUIPMENT
Large roasting tin or oven tray (about 40 x 30cm/16 x 12in)

4 skinless, boneless chicken thighs (about 150g each)

FOR THE HERB AND SPICE MARINADE

2 tsp smoked paprika
2 tsp garlic granules
2 tsp dried oregano
pinch of cayenne pepper

FOR THE ROASTED VEGETABLES

low-calorie cooking spray
400g new potatoes, cut in half lengthways (quartered if large)
2 medium red onions, peeled and each cut into 8 wedges
1 medium red pepper, deseeded and cut into chunky pieces
1 medium green pepper, deseeded and cut into chunky pieces
200g cherry tomatoes, halved
40g ready-sliced chorizo
50g pitted black olives
sea salt and freshly ground black pepper
2 tbsp roughly chopped flat-leaf parsley, to serve

TIP:

Make sure to use a roasting tin or oven tray that's large enough to accommodate all the ingredients in a single layer.

For flavour without any fuss, look no further than this lovely, all-in-one traybake that uses a medley of Spanish-inspired herbs and smoky spices. It starts with marinating chicken thighs in a home-mixed, mildly spiced rub, and then baking them in the oven with lots of colourful veggies, until they're tender and juicy. You'll have hardly any washing-up to worry about afterwards, so there's really no excuse not to give this one a whirl tonight!

Everyday Light ───────────────

Mix the herb and spice marinade ingredients in a small bowl. Make two or three cuts diagonally across the tops of the chicken thighs. Place the chicken on a plate and sprinkle over half of the herb and spice mixture, rubbing it into the cuts and over all sides. Leave to marinate, covered in the fridge, for 30 minutes.

Preheat the oven to 220°C (fan 200°C/gas mark 7).

Spray the large roasting tin or oven tray with low-calorie cooking spray. Add the marinated chicken, potatoes, red onion wedges and pepper pieces, nestling the vegetables around the chicken. Sprinkle the remaining herb and spice mixture over the vegetables and season the chicken and vegetables well with salt and pepper. Spray the chicken and vegetables with low-calorie cooking spray and roast in the oven for 30 minutes. Turn the vegetables halfway through and spoon the juices over the chicken. You may find you need to add a splash of water at this point, if it's drying out.

Remove from the oven and add the tomatoes (cut side up), the chorizo slices and olives. Return to the oven for a further 15–20 minutes or until the tomatoes are wrinkling around the edges and the chicken shows no sign of pinkness (and the juices run clear). Remove from the oven, sprinkle with chopped parsley and serve.

The dish will keep in the fridge for 1–2 days.

VEGGIE

USE VEGGIE RAVIOLI, MOZZARELLA AND ITALIAN HARD CHEESE

FREEZE ME

BATCH COOK

GLUTEN FREE

USE GF RAVIOLI

CHEESY RAVIOLI LASAGNE

🕐 **15 MINS** 🍲 **30 MINS** ✕ **SERVES 4**

PER SERVING:
584 KCAL /32G CARBS

SPECIAL EQUIPMENT
Large ovenproof dish
(about 18 x 27cm/7 x 10½in)

250g ricotta cheese
45g Parmesan, finely grated
300g fresh beef ragu ravioli

FOR THE TOMATO SAUCE
500g passata
1 tsp garlic granules
2 tsp dried Italian herbs

FOR THE TOP
125g reduced-fat mozzarella,
 torn into large pieces
15g Parmesan, finely grated
a few fresh basil leaves, to
 garnish
sea salt and freshly ground
 black pepper

TO ACCOMPANY
75g mixed salad
 (+ 15 kcal per serving)

This might just be our easiest and cheesiest lasagne ever! You'd never guess from the taste that we've used a cheeky hack to make this recipe as fuss-free as possible. Rather than making a separate meat sauce, we've grabbed some readymade beef ravioli and layered it up with passata and a creamy mixture of ricotta and Parmesan cheese. Not only does this keep the ingredients list (and the washing-up pile) to a minimum, it means you can dish up dinner in just 45 minutes.

Special Occasion —————————————

Preheat the oven to 200°C (fan 180°C/gas mark 6).

Place the ricotta and Parmesan in a bowl, season well with salt and pepper and stir well. Set aside while you make the tomato sauce.

Place the passata, garlic granules and Italian herbs in a bowl and season well with salt and pepper. Stir well. Spoon one third of the tomato sauce into the ovenproof dish and spread it out in a thin layer to cover the bottom of the dish.

Place half of the ricotta mixture on top of the tomato sauce, using a dessertspoon to place dollops of the mixture on the tomato sauce and roughly spreading it out with the back of the spoon. Place half of the ravioli on top of the ricotta, arranging them side by side in a single layer without leaving any gaps. Spoon half of the remaining tomato sauce over the ravioli and spread it out roughly with the back of the spoon. Spoon the remaining ricotta mixture over the tomato sauce and use the back of a spoon to roughly spread it out.

Add the remaining ravioli and arrange them side by side in a single layer without any gaps. Spoon over the remaining tomato sauce and spread it out roughly to cover the ravioli.

Scatter the torn mozzarella and grated Parmesan on top in an even layer and bake in the oven for 25–30 minutes until bubbling, golden on top and piping hot throughout. Scatter a few fresh basil leaves on top and serve.

The lasagne will keep in the fridge for up to 3 days.

TIPS:

We used meat-filled ravioli, but you can use any ravioli of your choice and experiment with different flavours.

If you've frozen the dish, when reheating after defrosting, you may need to add a splash of water if it has dried out a little.

TUNA, PEPPER *and* POTATO BAKE

🕐 **10 MINS**   🍲 **30 MINS**   ✕ **SERVES 4**

PER SERVING:
351 KCAL / 37G CARBS

SPECIAL EQUIPMENT
30cm (12in) shallow casserole dish, suitable for oven and hob

low-calorie cooking spray
1 onion, peeled and thinly sliced
2 peppers (mixed colours), deseeded and thinly sliced
600g new potatoes, cut into 2cm (¾in) chunks
500ml stock (1 chicken, vegetable or fish stock cube dissolved in 500ml boiling water)
1 tsp mustard powder
1 tsp garlic granules
125g reduced-fat spreadable cheese
80g reduced-fat mature Cheddar, finely grated
50g wholemeal bread, blitzed into crumbs
handful of curly parsley, chopped
1 tbsp freshly squeezed lemon juice
2 x 145g tins tuna chunks in spring water, drained (drained weight should be 102g per tin)
freshly ground black pepper

TIP:
If you don't have a grill, preheat the oven to 220°C (fan 200°C/gas mark 7) and cook for 10–15 minutes, until the topping is crisp and golden.

Save yourself a trip to the shops and make this trusty, crowd-pleasing bake with tinned tuna chunks from your store cupboard. We've brought the flavours to life with chopped onion, peppers, zesty lemon juice and punchy reduced-fat Cheddar. You'll want to use new potatoes; they'll hold their shape even after cooking, making every bite all the more satisfying. For a moreish golden crunch, let it bake for a final 5 minutes with a blend of gloriously cheesy breadcrumbs on top.

Everyday Light ────────────

Spray the casserole dish with low-calorie cooking spray and place over a medium heat. Add the onion and peppers and cook for 5 minutes, until beginning to soften, then add the potatoes and stir in the stock. Bring to the boil, then cover and reduce the heat to a strong simmer. Cook for 15 minutes, stirring halfway through.

After 15 minutes, reduce the heat, add the mustard powder, garlic granules and spreadable cheese, stirring until it is melted. Increase the heat and let it bubble rapidly for 5–6 minutes, until the sauce has reduced a little and thickened to the consistency of single cream.

While the sauce reduces, preheat the grill to medium and mix half the grated Cheddar with the breadcrumbs and chopped parsley.

Turn off the hob heat and stir in the remaining Cheddar, lemon juice and drained tuna chunks and season with black pepper. Sprinkle the breadcrumb topping over the dish and place under the grill for 5 minutes, or until crisp and golden. Serve.

The dish will keep in the fridge for up to 3 days. To reheat from frozen, defrost (see guidance on page 11), then reheat, loosely covered in the microwave for 3–4 minutes, stirring halfway through, until piping hot. Place into an ovenproof dish and continue with the last step in the recipe above.

SUMAC SALMON *and* BULGUR WHEAT BAKE

🕐 **10MINS**   🍲 **35 MINS**   ✕ **SERVES 4**

PER SERVING:
560 KCAL /52G CARBS

SPECIAL EQUIPMENT
Ovenproof dish or roasting tray
(about 28 x 20cm/11 x 8in)

250g courgettes, cut into 1cm
   (½in)-thick half-moon shapes
1 red onion, peeled and cut into
   chunks
2 garlic cloves, peeled and
   crushed
low-calorie cooking spray
4 x 120g salmon fillets, skin
   removed
1 tbsp sumac
200g bulgur wheat, rinsed and
   drained
1 x 400g tin chickpeas, drained
   and rinsed
400ml hot vegetable stock
   (1 vegetable stock cube
   dissolved in 400ml boiling
   water)
juice of 1 lemon
handful of fresh dill, chopped
handful of fresh flat-leaf
   parsley, chopped
sea salt and freshly ground
   black pepper
lemon wedges, to serve
   (*optional*)

This Sumac Salmon and Bulgur Wheat Bake serves up bold, fresh, citrusy flavours for next to no effort. Inspired by Middle Eastern cuisine, we've combined lemon with tangy sumac, to guarantee that our dish packs the perfect punch. A yummy, low-fuss midweek dinner, you'll boost the dish by baking the salmon fillets on a fluffy bed of bulgur wheat, chickpeas and juicy, oven-roasted courgettes. Finish with extra herbs and a dash of lemon for even more zesty goodness!

Special Occasion ────────────

Preheat the oven to 220°C (fan 200°C/gas mark 7).

Put the courgettes, onion and garlic in the oven dish or roasting tray, mix together and spray well with low-calorie cooking spray. Place in the centre of the oven and roast for 20 minutes.

While the veg roasts, dust the salmon fillets with the sumac and season with salt and pepper.

After 20 minutes, remove the dish from the oven. Add the bulgur wheat, along with the chickpeas and hot stock. Stir in the lemon juice and season with a little salt and pepper if you wish. Lay the dusted salmon fillets on top and return to the oven for 15 minutes. The salmon should be cooked through and the bulgur wheat should have absorbed the stock until fluffy.

Remove from the oven, sprinkle over the chopped herbs and serve with extra lemon wedges, if using.

TIP:

Make sure the stock is hot before pouring it into the dish, otherwise the cooking time will be longer.

BAKES *and* ROASTS

173

PEANUT CHICKEN *and* SWEET POTATO TRAYBAKE

🕐 **10 MINS***   🍲 **40 MINS**   ✕ **SERVES 4**

*PLUS 30 MINS MARINATING

PER SERVING:
447 KCAL /38G CARBS

SPECIAL EQUIPMENT
Large baking tray (about 40 x 30cm/16 x 12in)

4 chicken legs (about 180g each)
2 tbsp plant-based coconut drink
600g sweet potatoes, scrubbed and cut into 4cm (1½in) chunks
low-calorie cooking spray
350g head of broccoli, cut into florets
sea salt and freshly ground black pepper

FOR THE MARINADE
2 tbsp smooth peanut butter
2 tbsp dark soy sauce
juice of 1 lime
1 tsp runny honey
1 tsp sriracha
1 garlic clove, peeled and crushed
2cm (¾in) piece of root ginger, peeled and grated

You can't beat the convenience of this Peanut Chicken and Sweet Potato Traybake. Even after a long, busy day, you'll always have the energy for the minimal chopping and mixing this faff-free recipe needs. Coat your chicken legs in the scrummy, satay-inspired marinade, chop your favourite veggies (we've gone for broccoli and sweet potatoes), and let your oven do the hard work for you.

Weekly Indulgence ——————————————

Mix the marinade ingredients together in a small bowl.

Rub half of the marinade into the chicken legs. It is not necessary to remove the skin, but you can if you wish. Put the legs on a plate and cover, then place in the fridge and allow to marinate for at least 30 minutes. You can marinate overnight, if you wish.

Mix the plant-based coconut drink into the remaining marinade to make a sauce. Cover and store in the fridge.

Preheat the oven to 220°C (fan 200°C/gas mark 7).

Arrange the sweet potato chunks in an even layer, down one side of the baking tray, spray with low-calorie cooking spray and season with salt and pepper. Place the marinated chicken legs down the other side, leaving a gap in between. Bake in the oven for 25 minutes.

After 25 minutes, remove from the oven. Toss the sweet potatoes around with a fish slice to ensure even cooking. Add the broccoli florets to the gap in between the chicken and sweet potatoes. Spray with low-calorie cooking spray and season with salt and pepper.

Return to the oven for a further 15 minutes, or until the chicken is thoroughly cooked. The juices should run clear and there should be no pink remaining. Divide among plates and drizzle the peanut sauce over before serving.

TIP:
We don't peel our sweet potatoes, but you can if you want.

BAKES *and* ROASTS

CHEESY BUTTERNUT *and* BACON ORZO

🕐 **20 MINS**   🍲 **45 MINS**   ✕ **SERVES 4**

PER SERVING:
419 KCAL /53G CARBS

SPECIAL EQUIPMENT
Large, deep frying pan
(about 30cm/12in)

low-calorie cooking spray
650g peeled and deseeded butternut squash, cut into 2cm (¾in) dice
1 medium onion, peeled and diced
250g white mushrooms, thickly sliced
2 tsp garlic granules
4 smoked bacon medallions, cut into 1–2cm (½–¾in) dice
½ tsp mustard powder
1 tsp dried thyme
1 tsp dried oregano
600ml chicken stock (1 very low-salt chicken stock cube dissolved in 600ml boiling water)
200g dried orzo
120g reduced-fat mature Cheddar, finely grated
2 tbsp roughly chopped flat-leaf parsley
freshly ground black pepper

Sweet butternut squash, salty bacon and mellow mushrooms give this wholesome pasta recipe a delicious, deep flavour. We love using tiny orzo pasta instead of rice, simmering it in chicken stock and melting in reduced-fat Cheddar, until you're left with a creamy, cheesy risotto-like dish. A perfect midweek meal, this one-pot wonder freezes like a dream. Do yourself a favour and make a few extra portions to stash away in the freezer for a rainy day!

Weekly Indulgence

Spray the large, deep frying pan with low-calorie cooking spray and place over a medium heat. Add the butternut squash and onion and cook for 10–15 minutes, until the butternut squash is beginning to lightly brown, and the onion is softened and golden. Add the mushrooms, garlic granules, bacon, mustard powder, thyme and oregano, stir well and cook for a further 10 minutes over a medium heat, until the bacon is cooked.

Add the chicken stock and bring to the boil, then add the orzo to the pan and stir well, ensuring the pasta is covered by the liquid. Reduce the heat to a simmer, cover with a lid and cook gently for 15–20 minutes, stirring frequently to make sure it doesn't stick to the pan.

The butternut squash should be soft inside, the orzo should be tender and most of the cooking liquid should have been absorbed. If there is still excess liquid, continue cooking, uncovered, for a few minutes longer.

The mixture should have a similar consistency to a risotto. Stir in the grated cheese until it has melted and is evenly combined. Stir in the chopped parsley and season with black pepper if needed. Serve hot.

The dish will keep in the fridge for up to 2 days.

TIP:
We find the bacon makes this dish salty enough, so we don't season with salt, only freshly ground black pepper.

CHICKEN, TOMATO *and* POTATO BAKE

🕐 **15 MINS**   🍲 **40 MINS**   ✕ **SERVES 4**

PER SERVING:
384 KCAL / 35G CARBS

SPECIAL EQUIPMENT
28cm (11in) shallow casserole dish, suitable for oven and hob

low-calorie cooking spray
500g diced chicken breast
1 onion, peeled and diced
2 red peppers, deseeded and diced
1 courgette, cut into 2cm (¾in) dice
4 garlic cloves, peeled and crushed
1 tsp dried oregano
1 tbsp tomato puree
1 x 400g tin chopped tomatoes
300ml chicken stock (1 chicken stock cube dissolved in 300ml boiling water)
2 tsp red wine vinegar
500g floury potatoes, peeled and cut into 2cm (¾in) dice
80g reduced-fat mature Cheddar, finely grated
sea salt and freshly ground black pepper

TO ACCOMPANY *(optional)*
75g mixed salad (+ 15 kcal per serving)

The inspiration for this easy-peasy, comforting dish comes from a local Turkish restaurant. The flavours in their chicken tava were so rich and warming, we made it our mission to recreate it – with a Pinch of Nom twist! You don't need fancy ingredients to make this simple meal, just chicken, a few vegetables and trusty store-cupboard staples. Let them simmer until your kitchen smells too good to leave, and you're ready to serve. To make it even cosier, we've given it a grilled cheese topping.

Everyday Light

Spray the casserole dish with low-calorie cooking spray and place over a medium heat. Add the chicken and onion and cook for 5 minutes, then add the peppers and courgette, garlic and oregano and cook for a further minute. Stir in the tomato puree, chopped tomatoes, stock and red wine vinegar. Add the potatoes and bring to the boil, then reduce the heat to a simmer, cover and cook for 20 minutes, stirring occasionally to ensure even cooking.

When the potatoes and chicken are fully cooked, turn off the hob and preheat the grill to medium.

Taste the sauce and season with salt and pepper if you wish. Sprinkle the cheese over the top then place under the grill for a couple of minutes until bubbling and golden.

Serve!

The dish will keep in the fridge for up to 2 days.

TIP:
If you don't have a grill, preheat the oven to 220°C (fan 200°C/gas mark 7) and cook the dish for 15 minutes.

BAKES *and* ROASTS

SLOW COOKER CAJUN-STYLE CHICKEN THIGHS

🕐 **15 MINS**   🍲 **2½–3 HRS**   ✕ **SERVES 2**

FREEZE ME

BATCH COOK

DAIRY FREE

GLUTEN FREE
USE GF STOCK CUBE

PER SERVING:
470 KCAL /47G CARBS

SPECIAL EQUIPMENT
3.5-litre slow cooker

4 skinless, boneless chicken
  thighs (about 380g in total)
low-calorie cooking spray
300g new potatoes, cut in half
¼ red pepper, deseeded and
  cut into 2cm (¾in) dice
¼ green pepper, deseeded and
  cut into 2cm (¾in) dice
1 red onion, peeled and sliced
3 garlic cloves, peeled and
  crushed
1 x 400g tin chopped tomatoes
150ml boiling water
1 chicken stock cube
1 tbsp tomato puree
1 tsp white granulated
  sweetener

FOR THE SPICE RUB
1 tbsp Cajun spice mix
½ tbsp sweet smoked paprika
2 tsp garlic granules
2 tsp onion granules
1 tsp dried oregano
¼ tsp salt
¼ tsp freshly ground black
  pepper

A handful of simple store-cupboard spices transforms this wholesome meal of chicken thighs, potatoes and vegetables into a dinner you'll look forward to all day long. The good news is you can leave your ingredients to bubble away in the slow cooker for hours and come home to a kitchen that smells irresistible. The chopped tomatoes cook down into a flavour-packed sauce that works a treat with the fall-off-the-fork, tender chicken thighs and filling new potatoes.

Weekly Indulgence

Combine the spice rub ingredients in a small bowl, then rub the mix into the chicken thighs until coated. Spray a frying pan with low-calorie cooking spray and place over a medium heat. Add the chicken thighs and fry for 3–4 minutes until browned on all sides.

Put the potatoes, peppers, onion, garlic, chopped tomatoes, water, chicken stock cube, tomato puree and sweetener in the slow cooker pot and stir well. Lay the chicken thighs on top of the vegetables, cover with the lid and cook on low for 2–3 hours. The chicken should be cooked through, with no signs of pinkness, and the vegetables should be soft. Serve.

IF YOU DON'T HAVE A SLOW COOKER
Alternatively, cook this in the oven. Preheat the oven to 180°C (fan 160°C/gas mark 4). Follow the steps above, adding everything to a casserole dish. Cover with a lid and cook in the oven for 45 minutes to 1 hour, stirring occasionally. The vegetables should be soft and the chicken thighs cooked through.

BAKES and ROASTS

HARISSA PILAF

 15 MINS   30 MINS   ✕ SERVES 4

PER SERVING:
438 KCAL / 65G CARBS

SPECIAL EQUIPMENT
Ovenproof dish (about 30 x 20cm/12 x 8in)

250g basmati rice
3 garlic cloves, peeled and crushed
2 vegetable stock cubes
4 tbsp medium harissa paste
2 tsp sweet smoked paprika
2 tsp mild chilli powder
½ tsp salt
½ tsp freshly ground black pepper
1 medium red onion, peeled and diced
1 medium red pepper, deseeded and diced
1 medium courgette, diced
1 x 400g tin chickpeas, drained and rinsed
40g pine nuts
600ml boiling water

TO ACCOMPANY *(optional)*
75g mixed salad
(+ 15 kcal per serving)

A hearty dish of rice, vegetables and chickpeas, we've spiced up this simple pilaf with a few spoonfuls of warming harissa paste. The North African-inspired seasoning adds a lovely smoky flavour, and we've thrown in some extra chilli powder to make it just a little bit more fiery (you can leave this out if you prefer!). Ideal for a midweek meal, you'll want to make this vegan-friendly dish time and time again.

Weekly Indulgence

Preheat the oven to 220°C (fan 200°C/gas mark 7).

Place the rice in a sieve and rinse under cold running water until the water runs clear. Leave to drain.

Add the garlic, stock cubes, harissa, paprika, chilli powder, salt and black pepper to the boiling water and stir until the stock cubes have dissolved.

Add the rice, onion, red pepper, courgette and chickpeas to the ovenproof dish and stir. Pour over the stock mixture and stir to combine, then cover the dish with foil and cook in the oven for 30 minutes or until the rice is cooked.

While the rice is cooking, put the pine nuts in a small frying pan and place over a medium heat. Lightly toast the pine nuts for a few minutes until lightly golden brown.

Once the rice is cooked, remove the dish from the oven, remove the foil, sprinkle over the pine nuts and lightly stir. Serve!

The dish will keep for up to 1 day in the fridge.

TIP:
If freezing, defrosting and reheating, don't reheat more than once. See guidelines on page 11.

BAKES *and* ROASTS

USE GF
SOY SAUCE

SPICY PORK *and* ROAST POTATOES

🕐 **5 MINS**   🍲 **45 MINS**   ✕ **SERVES 4**

PER SERVING:
357 KCAL / 28G CARBS

SPECIAL EQUIPMENT
Large casserole dish, suitable for oven and hob

low-calorie cooking spray
600g baby potatoes, cut in half lengthways
½ tsp paprika
¼ tsp dried chilli flakes
500g lean diced pork
250g broccoli, cut into florets
1 tsp sesame seeds, to garnish

FOR THE SAUCE
2 garlic cloves, peeled and crushed
2 tsp cider vinegar
1 tbsp dark soy sauce
1 tsp medium chilli powder
1 tsp smooth peanut butter
1 tbsp light sweet chilli sauce
1 tsp toasted sesame oil

Inspired by some of our favourite Asian-style flavours, this is a simple combination of pork, potatoes and broccoli that's a whole meal in one dish. It may be low on effort, but don't be fooled into thinking that means it's lacking in oomph! There's plenty of spice and sweet chilli sauce to give this recipe a good kick, although you can easily make it milder if you prefer.

Everyday Light

Preheat the oven to 190°C (fan 170°C/gas mark 5).

Spray the casserole dish with low-calorie cooking spray and place over a medium heat. Put the halved baby potatoes into the dish, cut side down, and fry for about 5 minutes until they start to colour. Once they are starting to go golden, flip them over and sprinkle them with the paprika and chilli flakes. Leave to cook for another couple of minutes.

While the potatoes are browning, make the sauce.

Put the sauce ingredients in a bowl and mix well until smooth.

Once the potatoes are browned, turn off the heat and add the pork and sauce in between the potatoes. Scatter over the broccoli florets, stir well, and bake in the oven for 30–35 minutes, until the pork and potatoes are cooked through. The pork should show no sign of pinkness inside.

Remove from the oven and serve with a sprinkling of sesame seeds!

The dish will keep in the fridge for up to 3 days.

TIP:
You can make this as spicy or as mild as you like – just add more or less of the chilli flakes and chilli powder!

VEGGIE

USE VEGGIE CHICKEN AND SAUSAGES, USE VEGGIE STOCK CUBE

FREEZE ME

BATCH COOK

CREAMY CHICKEN COBBLER

🕐 **20 MINS**　　🍲 **50 MINS**　　✕ **SERVES 4**

PER SERVING:
528 KCAL / 60G CARBS

SPECIAL EQUIPMENT
Large casserole dish with a tight-fitting lid (about 28cm/11in), suitable for oven and hob

low-calorie cooking spray
350g diced chicken breast
3 reduced-fat pork sausages, cut into 4 pieces
1 onion, peeled and diced
2 carrots, peeled and sliced
a few fresh sage leaves, roughly chopped
400ml chicken stock (1 chicken stock cube dissolved in 400ml boiling water)
200g new potatoes, thinly sliced
150g frozen peas
50g reduced-fat cream cheese
1 tbsp cornflour, mixed to a slurry with 1 tbsp water

FOR THE COBBLER TOPPING
180g self-raising flour
¼ tsp baking powder
40g reduced-fat spread
a few fresh sage leaves, finely chopped
1 tsp onion granules
a good pinch of salt
4 tbsp skimmed milk

Typically topped with scone-like crumbly biscuits, a cobbler is a tried and trusted winter warmer. You've probably heard of sweet, fruity cobbler before, but savoury versions like this one seem to be less common – we think they deserve to be more popular! We simmer chicken and sausages in a mild, creamy sauce (with no real cream in sight), and we can't get enough of the rustic sage and onion topping; just wait until it crisps up and turns golden in the oven.

Special Occasion ————————————

Spray the casserole dish with low-calorie cooking spray and place over a medium heat. Add the chicken and sausage pieces and cook for 6–8 minutes, stirring until they start to colour. Add the onion, carrots and sage and cook for 8 minutes until everything is golden brown, then add the stock and potato slices. Bring to the boil, then reduce the heat to a simmer, cover and cook for 10 minutes while you prepare the cobbler topping.

Preheat the oven to 200°C (fan 180°C/gas mark 6).

Sift the flour and baking powder together into a bowl and add the reduced-fat spread. Rub together with clean fingertips until the mix resembles breadcrumbs, then stir in the sage, onion granules and salt. Mix in the milk a little at a time, until it forms a dough. If you need any more liquid, add a few drops of cold water.

When the potatoes and carrots are just cooked, add the frozen peas, then stir in the cream cheese until completely blended. Stir in the cornflour slurry and simmer for a few minutes, stirring until thickened. Remove from the heat.

Now take the cobbler topping and tear it roughly into pieces, then place evenly over the top of the filling. Bake in the oven for 20 minutes, or until the topping is golden and cooked through.

Remove from the oven and serve.

The dish will keep in the fridge for up to 2 days.

BAKES and ROASTS

PEA, POTATO *and* ONION FRITTATA

🕐 **5 MINS**   🍲 **25 MINS**   ✕ **SERVES 4**

VEGGIE

FREEZE ME

BATCH COOK

DAIRY FREE
USE DF CHEESE ALTERNATIVE

GLUTEN FREE

PER SERVING:
312 KCAL /20G CARBS

SPECIAL EQUIPMENT
28cm (11in) non-stick ovenproof
frying pan or shallow, round hob-safe casserole dish

low-calorie cooking spray
1 onion, peeled and sliced
1 garlic clove, peeled and crushed
150g frozen garden peas
1 x 567g tin new potatoes, drained (drained weight 345g) and cut into 5mm (¼in)-thick slices
8 large eggs
50g reduced-fat mature Cheddar, finely grated
handful of fresh basil leaves, roughly shredded
sea salt and freshly ground black pepper

TO ACCOMPANY
75g mixed salad
   (+ 15 kcal per serving)

TIP:
You can use leftover boiled or new potatoes instead of tinned. Use 345g and cut into 5mm (¼in)-thick slices or small dice.

Who doesn't love a frittata? So quick and easy to rustle up, this recipe makes the most of a handy store-cupboard ingredient: tinned new potatoes. Ideal when you've got a hankering for spuds without the faff, we've also thrown in fresh-tasting peas, basil and sliced onion. Served hot or cold, this one's sure to fill you up in a jiffy, and it'll stay nice and cheesy in your lunchbox for the next day too.

Everyday Light ———————————

Preheat the oven to 220°C (fan 200°C/gas mark 7).

Spray the ovenproof frying pan with low-calorie cooking spray and place over a medium heat. Add the onion and garlic and fry for 5 minutes until the onion has softened, then add the frozen peas and the potatoes and cook for 3 minutes until heated through.

While the vegetables are cooking, beat the eggs together with half the grated cheese and some salt and pepper. Stir the shredded basil through the eggs.

When the potatoes and peas are heated through, pour the egg mixture into the pan. Stir gently with a spatula for 2–3 minutes, until the eggs begin to set on the bottom, then sprinkle the remaining cheese on top and place in the oven.

Cook for 10–12 minutes, or until the eggs are set and the frittata is cooked through.

Cut into 4 wedges and serve, hot or cold, with mixed salad: we've used this accompaniment to ensure this is a true, all-in-one recipe. You can enjoy this dish with any accompaniment you like, but don't forget to adjust the calories accordingly.

The frittata will keep in the fridge for up to 3 days. For freezing and defrosting guidance see page 11.

BAKES *and* ROASTS

SLOW COOKER CHICKEN WITH APRICOTS

🕐 **15 MINS**   🍲 **4½–5 HRS**   ✕ **SERVES 4**

PER SERVING:
416 KCAL /39G CARBS

SPECIAL EQUIPMENT
3.5-litre slow cooker

8 skinless, boneless chicken
  thighs (about 650g in total)
low-calorie cooking spray
1 medium red onion, peeled and
  thinly sliced
1 yellow pepper, deseeded and
  sliced
1 red pepper, deseeded and
  sliced
2 carrots, peeled and sliced
3 garlic cloves, peeled and
  crushed
1 x 400g tin chopped tomatoes
240g tinned chickpeas, drained
  and rinsed
100ml boiling water
1 chicken stock cube
2 tbsp tomato puree
1 tbsp white granulated
  sweetener
80g dried apricots, sliced

FOR THE SPICE RUB
2 tsp smoked paprika
1 tsp ground cumin
1 tsp ground coriander
1 tsp garlic granules
1 tsp onion powder
½ tsp turmeric
½ tsp ground cinnamon
½ tsp ground ginger

Inspired by the fragrant flavours of North African cooking, this tagine-style meal is made in your slow cooker, rather than an earthenware pot. Packed with chicken and chickpeas, there's lots of protein in this dish, which is great for keeping you feeling fuller for longer. If you're super organised, you can even prep all the ingredients the night before, pop them in the slow cooker pot and refrigerate it until you're ready to cook. After simmering away all day, the tender chicken thighs will melt in your mouth, with a juicy pop of sweetness from the apricots.

Weekly Indulgence

Combine the spice rub ingredients in a small bowl, then rub the mix into the chicken thighs until well coated. Spray a frying pan with low-calorie cooking spray and place over a medium heat. Add the chicken thighs and fry for 3–4 minutes until browned on all sides.

Put the onion, peppers, carrot, garlic, chopped tomatoes and chickpeas in the slow cooker pot. In a jug, combine the water, chicken stock cube, tomato puree and sweetener. Stir well and pour it over the vegetables. Add the dried apricots and lay the chicken thighs on top. Cover with the lid and cook on low for 4½–5 hours. The chicken should be cooked with no signs of pinkness and the vegetables should be soft.

Serve and enjoy!

IF YOU DON'T HAVE A SLOW COOKER
Alternatively, cook this in the oven. Preheat the oven to 200°C (fan 180°C/gas mark 6). Follow the steps above and add everything to a large casserole dish. Cover with a lid and cook for 30–40 minutes until the chicken is cooked through and the vegetables are soft.

CAJUN-STYLE CHICKEN ORZO

🕐 **10 MINS***   🍲 **1 HR 5 MINS**   ✕ **SERVES 4**

*PLUS 10 MINS MARINATING

PER SERVING:
493 KCAL /59G CARBS

SPECIAL EQUIPMENT
Large ovenproof frying pan or casserole dish with tight-fitting lid (about 26cm/10in, suitable for oven and hob)

8 skinless, boneless chicken thigh fillets (visible fat removed), about 75g each
2 tbsp Cajun seasoning
low-calorie cooking spray
1 medium onion, peeled and cut into 1cm (½in) dice
6 garlic cloves, peeled and finely chopped
1 medium red pepper, deseeded and cut into 1cm (½in) dice
1 medium green pepper, deseeded and cut into 1cm (½in) dice
4 white mushrooms, thickly sliced
100g fine green beans, trimmed and halved
8 cherry tomatoes, halved
juice of 1 lemon
500ml chicken stock (1 chicken stock cube dissolved in 500ml boiling water)
250g dried orzo
1 x 198g tin sweetcorn in water, drained
handful of curly parsley, chopped, plus 1 tbsp extra chopped parsley to garnish (*optional*)
sea salt and freshly ground black pepper

There's no need for a side dish when this filling orzo recipe is on the menu! We've marinated juicy chicken thighs in a time-saving, low-faff, shop-bought spice blend, and then packed a rainbow of fresh vegetables in with our hearty orzo pasta. Everything can be left to bubble away in the oven, until it's ready for you to dish out and get stuck in.

Weekly Indulgence

Coat the chicken thigh fillets in the Cajun seasoning and set aside for 10 minutes.

Preheat the oven to 200°C (fan 180°C/gas mark 6).

Spray the large ovenproof frying pan or casserole dish with low-calorie cooking spray and place over a medium heat. Add the chicken thighs and cook for 4–5 minutes, until browned on all sides. Remove from the pan and set aside.

Spray the pan with more low-calorie cooking spray (no need to wash it first) and add the onion, garlic, peppers, mushrooms and green beans. Cook over a medium heat for 5–8 minutes, until the onions and peppers are softening, then add the cherry tomatoes, lemon juice and 100ml of the chicken stock. Stir, then return the chicken to the pan. Cover with a tight-fitting lid or tight-fitting kitchen foil and bake in the oven for 30 minutes.

Remove from the oven and add the orzo, sweetcorn, parsley and the remaining stock. Stir well, then return to the oven for 20 minutes, uncovered, stirring halfway through.

Taste and season with salt and pepper, if needed. Garnish with a little extra chopped parsley, if using, and serve.

TIP:
We would say this dish has a medium-spicy heat, but you can add a little more or less Cajun seasoning to suit your own taste.

VEGGIE

USE VEGGIE HALLOUMI

VEGAN

USE VEGAN HALLOUMI

FREEZE ME

OMIT THE YOGHURT AND BASIL TOPPING

BATCH COOK

DAIRY FREE

USE DF HALLOUMI AND YOGHURT

GLUTEN FREE

MEDITERRANEAN-STYLE HALLOUMI BAKE

🕐 **15 MINS**   🍲 **55 MINS**   ✕ **SERVES 4**

PER SERVING:
398 KCAL /37G CARBS

SPECIAL EQUIPMENT
Deep casserole dish (about 26cm/10in)

1 x 567g tin new potatoes in water, drained
1 x 400g tin butter beans in water, rinsed and drained
1 medium red onion, peeled and finely chopped
4 garlic cloves, peeled and crushed
1 red pepper, deseeded and cut into 1cm (½in) dice
1 green pepper, deseeded and cut into 1cm (½in) dice
low-calorie cooking spray
500g passata
2 tsp dried Italian herbs
225g reduced-fat halloumi, cut into 1cm (½in)-thick slices
12 cherry tomatoes, halved
8 pitted black olives
sea salt and freshly ground black pepper

FOR THE TOP
100g fat-free Greek yoghurt
a few fresh basil leaves, to garnish

TO ACCOMPANY *(optional)*
25g mini flatbread
(+ 78 kcal per flatbread)

A budget-friendly bake that's bursting with Mediterranean-inspired flavours? Yes please! You'll be pleasantly surprised with how easy it is to turn a tin of new potatoes and some butter beans into a filling family meal that everyone will love. Arrange slices of squishy, salty halloumi on the top and pop it into the oven until they've turned golden. Add a spoonful of Greek yoghurt and a few basil leaves for freshness, and you're good to go!

Everyday Light ────────────

Preheat the oven to 220°C (fan 200°C/gas mark 7).

Place the potatoes, butter beans, onion, garlic and peppers in the deep casserole dish. Spray with low-calorie cooking spray, season with salt and pepper and stir well. Take care not to add too much salt as the halloumi will add saltiness to the dish. Bake in the oven for 30–35 minutes, uncovered, until the potatoes are golden and the onion and peppers are soft. Stir halfway through.

Remove from the oven, add the passata and dried Italian herbs and stir to mix with the vegetables.

Arrange the halloumi slices, cherry tomatoes and olives on top, tucking the halloumi into the tomato sauce, then return to the oven and bake, uncovered, for a further 15–20 minutes, until bubbling and the halloumi is golden. Top with a dollop of yoghurt and a few fresh basil leaves. Serve, with mini flatbreads if you like.

The dish will keep in the fridge for 1–2 days (without the yoghurt and basil).

SLOW COOKER STUFFED PEPPERS

🕐 **15 MINS**   🍲 **3 HRS 10 MINS**   ✕ **SERVES 4**

VEGGIE

VEGAN
USE VEGAN CHEESE

DAIRY FREE
USE DF CHEESE

GLUTEN FREE

PER SERVING:
230 KCAL /26G CARBS

SPECIAL EQUIPMENT
3.5-litre slow cooker

4 medium peppers
150g dried quinoa
½ red onion, finely diced
70g drained tinned black beans, rinsed
70g drained tinned chickpeas, rinsed
3 garlic cloves, peeled and crushed
90g harissa paste
1 tbsp tomato puree
1 tsp mixed herbs
1 tsp garlic granules
200g passata
40g reduced-fat Cheddar cheese, finely grated
sea salt and freshly ground black pepper
10g coriander, chopped, to serve (*optional*)

TO ACCOMPANY
75g mixed salad (+ 15 kcal per serving)

TIPS:

We find using a spoon to remove the seeds, core and membrane of the peppers is a lot easier than a knife!

You can use tri-colour quinoa instead, if you prefer!

Flicking through on the hunt for a tasty lunch idea? Pop these Stuffed Peppers in your slow cooker. To make them into a tasty, nutritious meal, we've scooped them out and filled them to the brim with a combination of quinoa, chickpeas and black beans. You can count on this recipe to leave you feeling fuller for longer, thanks to all the protein-rich ingredients we've included! To give everything a kick, we've swirled through one of our favourite low-fuss, smoky ingredients: harissa paste. They work so well with coriander and a melty layer of cheese on top!

Everyday Light ———————————

Cut the tops off the peppers and remove the seeds, core and any membranes. Rinse the quinoa well in cold water and drain.

In a bowl, combine the quinoa, onion, black beans, chickpeas, garlic, harissa paste, tomato puree, mixed herbs, garlic granules and passata. Mix well and season with salt and pepper.

Stand the peppers in the slow cooker pot, fill with the quinoa mixture and pop the tops of the peppers back on top.

Pour 150ml of cold water into the slow cooker pot – the bottom of the peppers should just be covered with the water. Cover with the lid and cook on high for 3 hours. Remove the lid and top the peppers with the grated cheese, re-cover and cook for a further 10 minutes until the cheese is melted. Sprinkle over the chopped coriander, if using, and serve.

IF YOU DON'T HAVE A SLOW COOKER
Alternatively, cook these peppers in the oven. Preheat the oven to 210°C (fan 190°C/gas mark 7). Prepare the peppers and quinoa mixture as above, then stand the peppers on a baking tray or casserole pan and fill with the quinoa mixture. Cover with foil or a lid and bake for 30–40 minutes, until the peppers are soft, and the quinoa is cooked. Add the cheese and cook for a further 5–10 minutes until melted.

BAKES and ROASTS

LANCASHIRE HOTPOT

🕐 **15 MINS**   🍲 **2½ HRS**   ✕ **SERVES 4**

PER SERVING:
560KCAL /51G CARBS

SPECIAL EQUIPMENT
**Deep casserole dish
(about 26cm/10in)**

2 onions, peeled and diced
8 carrots, peeled and diced
800g diced lamb, all visible fat
   removed
800g floury potatoes, peeled
   and thinly sliced
400ml lamb, chicken, vegetable
   or beef stock (1 stock cube
   dissolved in 400ml boiling
   water)
sea salt and freshly ground
   black pepper

There's something about making a dish from your childhood
that brings extra comfort, especially on a chilly, grey day.
This simple Lancashire Hotpot recipe has been passed down
through generations, and the only change we've made
is that we now remove all of the fat from the lamb before
cooking. It doesn't get much more classic than this – turning
hearty, wholesome ingredients into a home-cooked meal
that'll gather the whole family around the table together.

Special Occasion

Preheat the oven to 190°C (fan 170°C/gas mark 5).

Place the onions and carrots in the casserole dish, add
the diced lamb on top of the vegetables and arrange the
potato slices neatly on top. Try to make sure there are no
gaps. Pour the stock all over the potatoes, then season with
a little salt and pepper. Cover with foil or the casserole lid
and cook in the oven for about 1½ hours.

Test to see if the potatoes and lamb are cooked. If not,
leave the dish in the oven (still covered) for a bit longer.

Remove the lid or foil and cook for another 40–50 minutes
or until the potato is crisp and golden, then serve.

The hotpot will keep in the fridge for up to 3 days.

BAKES *and* ROASTS

PORK *and* APPLE MEATLOAF *with* SAGE *and* ONION ROASTIES

🕐 **15 MINS**   🍲 **50 MINS**   ✕ **SERVES 4**

PER SERVING:
394 KCAL /40G CARBS

SPECIAL EQUIPMENT
30 x 26cm (12 x 10in) baking tray

500g floury potatoes, peeled and cut into 2.5cm (1in) cubes
low-calorie cooking spray
2 tsp onion granules
1 tsp dried sage
150g trimmed green beans
sea salt and freshly ground pepper

FOR THE MEATLOAF
500g 5%-fat minced pork
½ onion, peeled and finely chopped
1 garlic clove, peeled and crushed
5 fresh sage leaves, finely chopped, plus a few extra for garnish
60g wholemeal bread, blitzed into crumbs
1 eating apple
1 medium egg
2 tbsp milk (we used skimmed, but you can use whichever you have in your fridge!)
1 tsp wholegrain mustard
1 tsp runny honey
½ tsp balsamic vinegar

You've never made meatloaf as simple as this! It comes ready-portioned into impressive-looking mini meatloaves, with a gorgeous golden side of roast potatoes and crunchy green beans. Juicy apples and pork make for a heavenly combination, which is why we've added an infusion of grated apple, and a garnish of slices on top of each loaf. The tangy mustard glaze takes this roasted spread to the next level, so you'll be left with a hearty family meal, and next to no washing-up to think about afterwards.

Everyday Light ───────────

Preheat the oven to 200°C (fan 180°C/gas mark 6).

Rinse the potatoes in cold water and pat dry. Place in a bowl and spray well with low-calorie cooking spray.

Sprinkle over the onion granules and dried sage, and season with salt and pepper. Toss until the potatoes are well coated, scatter evenly over the baking tray, place in the oven and cook for 25 minutes.

While the potatoes are cooking, make the meatloaf.

Put the pork, onion, garlic, fresh sage and breadcrumbs in a mixing bowl.

Cut the apple into quarters and peel 3 of them. Remove the core and grate the three peeled quarters into the pork mixture. Add the egg and milk, season well with salt and pepper and mix until well combined. It's easiest to use your hands for this, but you can use a spoon and a bit more effort, if you wish. Divide the pork mixture into 4 equal portions and shape into mini meatloaves, around 5cm (2in) high.

Slice the remaining quarter of the apple into 12 thin slices and place 3 slices on top of each mini meatloaf.

After 25 minutes, remove the potatoes from the oven. Using a fish slice, toss them around and push them towards one

end of the tray. Place the meatloaves at the other end. Spray the tops with low-calorie cooking spray and return to the oven for 15 minutes.

While the meatloaves cook, mix the wholegrain mustard, honey and balsamic vinegar together in a small bowl to make a glaze.

After 15 minutes, remove the tray from the oven. Brush the honey and mustard glaze evenly over each meatloaf, using a pastry brush. If you don't have a brush, you can use a teaspoon to drizzle the glaze over the top. Push the meatloaves up to make some space at the end of the tray, add the green beans, spray them with low-calorie cooking spray and season with salt and pepper.

Return to the oven for 10 minutes or until the meatloaves are cooked through, the potatoes are golden and soft in the middle and the green beans are cooked, with a crunchy bite.

Serve.

TIPS:

You can freeze the meatloaves once cooked: cool quickly and wrap well before freezing. Defrost overnight in a refrigerator. They are best reheated in a moderate oven for about 15 minutes or until piping hot throughout.

Alternatively, cover loosely and reheat in the microwave for about 4 minutes, turning them halfway through.

FREEZE
ME

BATCH
COOK

GLUTEN
FREE

USE GF
STOCK CUBE

HASSELBACK POTATO
and BACON BAKE

🕐 **10 MINS**   🍲 **1 HR 10 MINS**   ✕ **SERVES 4**

PER SERVING:
312 KCAL /33G CARBS

SPECIAL EQUIPMENT
18 x 27cm (7 x 10½in)
ovenproof
dish, heatproof jug

low-calorie cooking spray
4 medium potatoes, unpeeled
  and halved lengthways
  (about 160g each)
400ml hot chicken stock (1 very
  low-salt chicken stock cube
  dissolved in 400ml boiling
  water)
160g reduced-fat cream cheese
2 garlic cloves, peeled and
  crushed
80g reduced-fat mature
  Cheddar, finely grated
4 smoked bacon medallions,
  cut into 1cm (½in) dice
3 spring onions, thinly sliced
freshly ground black pepper

TO ACCOMPANY
75g mixed salad (+ 15 kcal per
serving). We've suggested
this accompaniment to ensure
this is a true, all-in-one recipe.
You can enjoy this dish with
any accompaniment but don't
forget to adjust the calories
accordingly.

These easy, cheesy potatoes are far lighter in calories than
you'd expect. Baked to perfection in a creamy, garlicky
sauce, we've sliced them 'hasselback' style to make sure
they soak up the flavours without losing their gorgeous
crispiness. Complete with a sprinkling of smoked bacon,
grated Cheddar and crunchy spring onions, this is the kind
of slimming-friendly dish dreams are made of!

Everyday Light ─────────────────────

Preheat the oven to 200°C (fan 180°C/gas mark 6) and grease
the ovenproof dish with a little low-calorie cooking spray.

Place the potato halves on a chopping board, flat side
down. Make narrow, evenly spaced cuts across the width of
each potato half, working from one end of the potato to the
other end. Cut as far into the potato halves as you can, but
don't cut right through.

Place the potato halves flat side down in the greased
ovenproof dish.

In a heatproof jug, mix the boiling hot stock, cream cheese
and garlic, and season well with pepper. Stir until the cream
cheese has completely dissolved and the mixture is smooth.

Pour the cream cheese and stock mixture over the potatoes
in the dish. They should be almost submerged, with just a
little of their tops visible.

Sprinkle over half of the grated Cheddar, half of the bacon
and two of the sliced spring onions. Cook in the oven,
uncovered, for 40 minutes, until the potatoes are just tender.

Remove from the oven and sprinkle with the remaining
Cheddar and bacon. Return to the oven and continue to
cook, uncovered, for a further 30 minutes, until the potatoes
are soft inside and the top is bubbling and golden.

Sprinkle the top with the remaining sliced spring onion and
serve with a mixed salad.

The dish will keep, covered, in the fridge for 1–2 days.

FREEZE ME

BATCH COOK

DAIRY FREE

GLUTEN FREE
USE GF STOCK POT

SLOW COOKER PORK POT ROAST

🕐 **20 MINS**   🍲 **4 HRS**   ✕ **SERVES 6**

PER SERVING:
380 KCAL /35G CARBS

SPECIAL EQUIPMENT
3.5-litre slow cooker, stick blender

2 tsp dried sage
2 tsp garlic granules
¼ tsp mustard powder
¼ tsp salt
¼ tsp freshly ground black pepper
1kg pork joint, any visible fat removed
low-calorie cooking spray
400g new potatoes, halved
3 medium carrots, peeled and cut into 2.5cm (1in)-thick slices
3 medium parsnips, peeled and cut into 2.5cm (1in)-thick slices
1 medium red onion, peeled and sliced
2 celery sticks, cut into 2.5cm (1in)-thick slices
4 garlic cloves, peeled and crushed
100ml boiling water
150ml apple juice
1 tbsp Henderson's relish
1 tbsp balsamic vinegar
1 tbsp tomato puree
2 tsp Dijon mustard
2 tbsp cornflour
1 tbsp white granulated sweetener
1 chicken stock pot

TIP:

If your gravy is a little thin, set the slow cooker to high with the lid off and continue to cook while the pork is resting.

Love a Sunday roast, but don't love all the effort it takes? Stick everything in your slow cooker! To double-up on gorgeous flavours, we've rubbed the pork joint with dried herbs, before simmering it in a lip-smacking combination of stock, apple juice and balsamic vinegar, with just a hint of Dijon mustard. All those ingredients mingle with the juices from the meat and the vegetables in the pot, ready to be turned into the easiest gravy you'll ever make – just scoop out the bigger veggies, then blend until it's thick and ready to pour.

Everyday Light

Combine the sage, garlic granules, mustard powder, salt and pepper in a small bowl and rub into the surface of the pork joint.

Spray a frying pan with low-calorie cooking spray and place over a medium heat. Add the pork and brown on all sides. Add the potatoes, carrot, parsnip, onion, celery and garlic to the slow cooker pot. Nestle the pork joint in the vegetables.

In a jug, combine the water, apple juice, Henderson's relish, balsamic vinegar, tomato puree, Dijon mustard, cornflour, sweetener and stock pot. Mix until smooth. Pour the stock mixture over the vegetables and pork. Cover with the lid and cook on high for 4 hours.

Lift the pork out of the slow cooker and leave it to rest on a plate for 10 minutes, covered in foil to keep it warm. Remove the larger veg with a slotted spoon and blitz the remaining stock and smaller vegetables with a stick blender until smooth.

Slice the pork and serve with vegetables and the gravy.

IF YOU DON'T HAVE A SLOW COOKER
Alternatively, cook this in the oven. Preheat the oven to 180°C (fan 160°C/gas mark 4). Follow the steps above, using 350ml boiling water and 400ml apple juice, place in a casserole dish and cover with a lid. Cook for 3–3½ hours, stirring halfway through. If your gravy is a little thin once blitzed, transfer to a pan and reduce.

BAKES *and* ROASTS

VEGGIE

USE VEGGIE
MOZZARELLA AND
VEGGIE COOKED
SLICED SAUSAGE

**FREEZE
ME**

**BATCH
COOK**

**DAIRY
FREE**

USE DF
CHEESES

**GLUTEN
FREE**

USE GF
PASTRY

PIZZA TART

🕐 **15 MINS**   🍲 **25 MINS***   ✕ **SERVES 4**

*PLUS 5 MINS COOLING

PER SERVING:
445 KCAL /36G CARBS

SPECIAL EQUIPMENT
Large baking tray (about 38 x
26cm/15 x 10in), pastry brush

320g ready-rolled light puff
  pastry sheet, about 35 x 26cm
  (14 x 9in)
1 medium egg, beaten

FOR THE TOP
4 tbsp tomato puree
2 garlic cloves, peeled and
  crushed
½ tsp dried basil
½ tsp dried oregano
40g reduced-fat mature
  Cheddar, finely grated
¼ small red onion, peeled and
  sliced into thin strips
8 thin slices of pepperoni
6 cherry tomatoes, halved
125g reduced-fat mozzarella,
  torn into pieces
8 pitted black olives
sea salt and freshly ground
  black pepper
a few fresh basil leaves,
  to serve

TO ACCOMPANY *(optional)*
75g mixed salad
  (+ 15 kcal per serving)

We've given pizza night a pastry twist with this easy-peasy
recipe! Instead of a dough base, we've worked wonders
with a sheet of ready-rolled light puff pastry. After pre-
baking the pastry, you can get creative with your toppings
– this pre-baking keeps it nice and crispy by the time your
pizza tart is baked to perfection. There are no rules when it
comes to toppings: try a different flavour combo every time
you make it (it's so tasty you'll definitely be making it more
than once!).

Weekly Indulgence

Preheat the oven to 220°C (fan 200°C/gas mark 7).

Unroll the pastry sheet and place it on the large baking tray,
still on the greaseproof paper packaging sheet. Use a large,
sharp knife to lightly score a line around the pastry sheet,
about 1cm (½in) in from the edge, taking care not to cut
right through the pastry. Use a fork to prick the centre of the
pastry sheet well, but not the edges.

Prick right through the pastry as this will prevent the pastry
rising too much. Brush beaten egg all over the pastry sheet,
including the edges. Place in the oven and bake 'blind' for
10 minutes until slightly risen and golden. Remove from the
oven and place the baking tray on a wire rack. Leave to
cool for about 5 minutes. During this time, the pastry will sink
to become flatter.

Meanwhile, put the tomato puree, garlic and dried herbs in
a small bowl. Season with salt and pepper and mix well.

Using the back of a spoon, spread the tomato puree mixture
over the centre of the pastry sheet in a thin layer.

Sprinkle the grated Cheddar over the tomato puree mixture
in a thin, even layer. Scatter the red onion over the cheese,
then arrange the pepperoni slices on top.

Place the cherry tomatoes cut side up on top of the tart. Add the torn mozzarella and black olives and bake in the oven for 10–12 minutes, until the cheeses have melted and are slightly golden.

Remove from the oven, scatter fresh basil leaves over the top and cut into 4 slices. Serve with mixed salad, if you like.

The pizza tart will keep in the fridge for up to 3 days. To freeze, place in a freezerproof container layered between sheets of non-stick baking paper to prevent the slices sticking together. Follow standard guidelines for defrosting on page 11 then reheat in a 220°C (fan 200C /gas mark 7) oven for about 5 minutes.

The pizza is not suitable for reheating in a microwave as the pastry will become soggy.

TIPS:

Prepare all the topping ingredients ahead so that you're prepared and ready to add them to the part-baked pastry base. Add them just before putting in the oven to make sure the pastry doesn't become soggy.

You can get creative and use topping ingredients of your own choice, but just avoid any ingredients that are too wet, otherwise you may find the pastry becomes soggy.

Remove the pastry from the fridge 5 minutes before unrolling.

FREEZE ME

BATCH COOK

GLUTEN FREE

USE GF GNOCCHI, STOCK CUBE AND BREADCRUMBS

SMOKED HADDOCK, SPINACH *and* GNOCCHI BAKE

🕐 **10 MINS**　🍲 **25 MINS**　✕ **SERVES 4**

PER SERVING:
402KCAL /43G CARBS

SPECIAL EQUIPMENT
Casserole dish (about 24cm/9in)

500g fresh gnocchi
100g baby spinach leaves
100g cherry tomatoes, halved
4 boneless, skinless smoked
  haddock fillets, about 120g
  each
125g reduced-fat mature
  Cheddar spreadable cheese
150ml fish stock (1 fish stock
  cube dissolved in 150ml
  boiling water)
150ml skimmed milk
½ tsp onion granules
½ tsp garlic granules
15g Parmesan, finely grated
1 tbsp wholegrain mustard
finely grated zest of ½ lemon

FOR THE TOPPING
15g panko breadcrumbs
15g Parmesan, finely grated
freshly ground black pepper

TO ACCOMPANY *(optional)*
75g mixed salad (+ 15 kcal per
  serving)

TIP:

If you've frozen the bake, when reheating after defrosting, you may need to add a splash of water if it has dried out a little in the freezer.

A tasty change from pasta, gnocchi are fluffy potato dumplings that you can boil, fry, or bake like we've done here. Paired with smoky fish and veggies, gnocchi make this a properly comforting, filling family meal. Haddock is naturally low-fat and low in calories, and works like a dream with our easy cheesy sauce. We've added plenty of spinach for green goodness, and sweet cherry tomatoes for a pop of colour. Topped off with a crunchy crumb, midweek meals don't come much easier than this.

Weekly Indulgence ───────────────

Preheat the oven to 220°C (fan 200°C/gas mark 7).

Place the gnocchi, spinach and tomatoes in the casserole dish and stir to combine.

Place the haddock fillets on top, nestling them in amongst the gnocchi and vegetables.

Add the spreadable cheese to the hot stock and stir until completely dissolved. Stir in the milk, onion granules, garlic granules, Parmesan, mustard and lemon zest and season with pepper. Pour the mixture over the gnocchi, spinach and tomatoes and place in the oven, uncovered, for 15 minutes.

Meanwhile, make the topping. Put the panko breadcrumbs and Parmesan in a small bowl, season with pepper and stir to combine. Set aside.

After 15 minutes, remove the casserole dish from the oven and gently stir the gnocchi and vegetables, taking care not to break up the fish. Sprinkle the panko and Parmesan mixture over the top and return to the oven for 5–10 minutes, or until bubbling and golden on top. The bake will be ready when the gnocchi is tender, the fish is flaky and opaque, and the sauce has thickened. Serve, with mixed salad alongside if you like. You can enjoy this dish with any accompaniment but don't forget to adjust the calories accordingly.

The bake will keep in the fridge for 1–2 days.

BAKES *and* ROASTS

SUNDAY ROAST CHICKEN TRAYBAKE

🕐 **10 MINS***   🍲 **1 HR 25 MINS**   ✕ **SERVES 4**

*PLUS 30 MINS SOAKING

PER SERVING:
434 KCAL / 36G CARBS

SPECIAL EQUIPMENT
Large baking tray with raised sides (about 38 x 26 x 2cm/15 x 10 x ¾in), heatproof jug

400g potatoes, peeled and cut into 3–4cm (1–1½in) chunks
3 medium carrots, peeled and cut into chunky sticks, about 6 x 1.5cm (2½ x ¾in)
2 medium parsnips, peeled and cut into chunky sticks, about 6 x 1.5cm (2½ x ¾in)
low-calorie cooking spray
4 large bone-in chicken thighs (skin and visible fat removed), about 170g each
½ tsp dried oregano
½ tsp dried thyme
½ tsp fine garlic granules
8 tenderstem broccoli spears
sea salt and freshly ground black pepper

FOR THE GRAVY
400ml hot beef or chicken stock (1 beef or chicken stock cube dissolved in 400ml boiling water)
2 tsp Worcestershire sauce or Henderson's relish
1 tsp 50%-less-sugar-and-salt tomato ketchup
½ tsp Dijon mustard
2 tsp cornflour, mixed to a slurry with 2 tsp water

We're not kidding when we say this Sunday Roast Chicken Traybake is a weekend gamechanger! Every bit of your next roast dinner can be cooked all on one baking tray – and that even includes the gravy. Don't skip the step of soaking the spuds in cold water; it helps remove the starch for fluffier roasties. The juicy chicken, tender veggies and fluffy potatoes taste so much better when you can enjoy them knowing there's hardly any cleaning up to do after you've eaten!

Weekly Indulgence ─────────

Put the potato chunks in a bowl of cold water and leave to soak for 30 minutes. We're not going to par-boil the potatoes before roasting them in this recipe, so this helps remove the starch and prevent them from having a sticky texture inside once roasted.

Drain the soaked potatoes and discard the starchy water. Rinse the potatoes under cold water, drain and dry well with kitchen paper. Preheat the oven to 210°C (fan 190°C/gas mark 7).

Place the dry potatoes, carrots and parsnips on the large baking tray, spray liberally with low-calorie cooking spray and season with salt and pepper. Toss to coat thoroughly. Roast the vegetables in the oven for about 35 minutes, turning them halfway through, until just tender inside and starting to brown a little around the edges.

While the vegetables are roasting, prepare the gravy. In a heatproof jug, mix the hot stock, Worcestershire sauce or Henderson's relish, tomato ketchup and Dijon mustard until combined. Set aside and leave to cool slightly.

Place the chicken thighs in between the vegetables on the tray and sprinkle the oregano, thyme and garlic granules over the surface of the chicken. Spray the vegetables and chicken liberally with low-calorie cooking spray and return to the oven for 30 minutes, turning the vegetables halfway through.

Add the tenderstem broccoli to the traybake and spray the broccoli with a little low-calorie cooking spray.

Return the tray to the oven for 5 minutes. The broccoli should still be crisp and green.

Pour the cornflour slurry into the slightly cooled gravy mixture and stir well. Pour the gravy mixture into the tray with the chicken, vegetables and their juices, return to the oven and cook for a further 10–15 minutes, until the gravy has bubbled and thickened slightly. The chicken should be thoroughly cooked and show no sign of pinkness, the potatoes, carrots and parsnips should be soft inside and golden brown on the outside, and the broccoli should be tender. Serve.

The dish will keep in the fridge for up to 2 days.

TIPS:

We use floury potatoes such as Maris Piper or King Edward as they will be soft and fluffy inside after roasting.

Cut the vegetables evenly and to a uniform size according to the dimensions stated. This will ensure everything is cooked properly in the timings given.

We remove the skin from the chicken thighs; you can leave it on if you prefer chicken with crispy skin (though you might want to pour the gravy mix around the chicken rather than over it, to keep the skin crisp). If you're concerned about calories, you will need to adjust them accordingly as this will increase the calories.

Make sure to use a large baking tray that has raised sides. It will need to be a minimum of 2cm (¾in) deep to contain the gravy and avoid spillages!

BAKED FETA, VEGETABLE *and* COUSCOUS TRAYBAKE

🕐 **15 MINS**　　🍲 **1 HR**　　✕ **SERVES 4**

PER SERVING:
483 KCAL /69G CARBS

SPECIAL EQUIPMENT
**32 x 24cm (12½ x 10in) oven
dish or roasting tray**

300g cherry tomatoes, halved
200g sweet potato, peeled and
　cut into 1cm (½in) dice
1 red onion, peeled and cut into
　wedges
1 red pepper, deseeded and
　diced
4 garlic cloves, peeled and
　crushed
good handful of fresh thyme,
　leaves stripped from their
　stalks (reserve a few whole
　sprigs for the top)
2 tbsp balsamic vinegar
low-calorie cooking spray
200g dried giant couscous
1 x 400g tin chickpeas, drained
　and rinsed
400ml hot vegetable stock
　(1 vegetable stock cube
　dissolved in 400ml boiling
　water)
200g reduced-fat feta cheese
sea salt and freshly ground
　black pepper

Giant couscous might look like a grain, but it's actually a type of pasta! For this effortless traybake, we've mixed it into sweet, balsamic-roasted vegetables and cooked it until it's silky and soft. Crumbled, reduced-fat feta cheese brings a creamy saltiness to balance the flavours, with fragrant thyme to top it all off. The best bit about this dish? It tastes incredible hot or cold – so you'll want to make sure you save the leftovers for lunch the next day.

Weekly Indulgence

Preheat the oven to 200°C (fan 180°C/gas mark 6).

Scatter the cherry tomatoes, sweet potato, red onion and pepper into the oven dish or roasting tray. Add the garlic, thyme leaves, balsamic vinegar and mix well. Spray well with low-calorie cooking spray and season with a little salt and pepper, then place in the oven and bake for 30 minutes, stirring halfway through.

After 30 minutes, add the couscous, chickpeas and hot stock. Stir well and return to the oven for 10 minutes.

After 10 minutes, remove from the oven and stir well.

Crumble the feta over the top, spritz with low-calorie cooking spray, scatter the reserved thyme sprigs on top and return to the oven for 15–20 minutes, until the couscous is tender and the feta is golden.

Remove from the oven and serve.

The dish will keep in the fridge for up to 3 days.

TIP:
You can replace fresh
thyme with ½ –1 teaspoon
of dried thyme.

VEGGIE

USE PLANT-
BASED MINCE

**FREEZE
ME**

RAW MEATBALLS
AND TOMATO
SAUCE ONLY

**DAIRY
FREE**

USE DF
CHEESE

**GLUTEN
FREE**

LAMB MEATBALL *and* SWEET POTATO TRAYBAKE

🕐 **20 MINS**　🍲 **1 HR 20 MINS**　✕ **SERVES 4**

PER SERVING:
333 KCAL / 28G CARBS

SPECIAL EQUIPMENT
27 x 22cm (10½ x 8½in) deep oven tray

FOR THE MEATBALLS
250g 10%-fat minced lamb
½ small red onion, peeled and finely chopped
1 garlic clove, peeled and crushed
1 tsp finely chopped fresh rosemary
¼ tsp ground sumac
1 small carrot, peeled and finely grated
1 medium egg, beaten

FOR THE TOMATO SAUCE AND VEGETABLES
low-calorie cooking spray
1 garlic clove, peeled and crushed
1 x 400g tin chopped tomatoes
1 tsp finely chopped rosemary, plus optional sprigs to serve
1 tbsp tomato puree
pinch of white granulated sweetener or sugar
350g sweet potatoes, peeled and cut into 1.5cm (¾in) chunks
2 medium courgettes, halved lengthways and cut into thick slices
120g cherry tomatoes, halved
100g reduced-fat feta, cut into cubes
sea salt and freshly ground black pepper

An easy-peasy, all-in-one dish that's bursting with Mediterranean-inspired flavours, our Lamb Meatball and Sweet Potato Traybake marries juicy lamb with a vibrant medley of tomatoey, oven-roasted veggies. It's simpler than you might think to get our homemade, rosemary-infused lamb meatballs prepped; you'll have them rolled and ready to bake to juicy perfection in less than 20 minutes. When everything's almost done, add a tangy layer of feta on top, and return to the oven until golden.

Everyday Light

Preheat the oven to 200°C (fan 180°C/gas mark 6).

To make the meatballs, mix the lamb, onion, garlic, rosemary, sumac and carrot in a bowl. Season with salt and pepper. Add the egg a little at a time until the mixture holds together well enough to form meatballs (you may not need to add all the egg). Form the lamb mixture into 8 evenly sized meatballs and set aside. (The meatballs can be frozen at this point, layered between sheets of non-stick baking paper in a freezerproof container, then defrosted before cooking in the sauce.)

To make the tomato sauce, place the garlic, chopped tomatoes, rosemary, tomato puree, a pinch of sweetener or sugar in a small bowl and season to taste with salt and pepper. Mix well..

Pour the tomato sauce into the deep baking tray. Add the sweet potatoes, courgettes and cherry tomatoes, scattering them over the tomato sauce. Place the meatballs on top of the vegetables, cover with foil and place in the oven for 1 hour, turning the meatballs once.

Remove the foil and scatter the feta over. Return to the oven for 15 minutes, until the meatballs are cooked and the cheese is beginning to turn lightly golden. Garnish with a sprig of rosemary, if you like, and serve.

The dish will keep in the fridge for up to 3 days.

BUTTERNUT SQUASH *and* RED ONION TARTE TATIN

🕐 **15 MINS***   🍲 **50 MINS****   ✕ **SERVES 4**

*PLUS 15 MINS CHILLING **PLUS 5 MINS RESTING

PER SERVING:
431 KCAL / 53G CARBS

SPECIAL EQUIPMENT
24cm (10in) ovenproof high-sided frying pan, suitable for use in the oven

375g ready-rolled light puff pastry sheet
400g peeled and deseeded butternut squash, cut into 5mm (¼in)-thick slices
low-calorie cooking spray
7g reduced-fat spread
2 medium red onions, peeled and thinly sliced
1 tbsp balsamic vinegar
½ tbsp runny honey
40g Greek-style salad cheese, crumbled
sea salt and freshly ground black pepper

TO ACCOMPANY
75g mixed salad
(+ 15 kcal per serving)

We've suggested this accompaniment to ensure this is a true, all-in-one recipe. You can enjoy this dish with any accompaniment you like, but don't forget to adjust the calories accordingly. The dish will keep in the fridge for up to 3 days.

With sliced butternut squash, honey and balsamic red onions, we think you'll agree that our upside-down tart is utterly delicious – whichever way you look at it! To keep the calories down without compromising on crispy comfort, we use reduced-fat puff pastry for the topsy-turvy base, and veggie-friendly, crumbled Greek-style salad cheese adds a punchy saltiness to our filling. Once you've carefully flipped your tarte, serve it with a side of salad or seasonal veg for a homely slice of autumn.

Weekly Indulgence ───────────

Preheat the oven to 200°C (fan 180°C/gas mark 6). Unroll the puff pastry sheet, leaving it on the greaseproof paper packaging sheet. Cut it into a disc that's slightly larger than the diameter of the frying pan and place it in the fridge for about 15 minutes while you make the filling.

Season the squash slices with salt and pepper. Spray the ovenproof high-sided frying pan with low-calorie cooking spray and place over a medium heat. Add the squash slices and cook for 10 minutes, turning them over halfway through cooking, or until cooked but firm and golden brown. Set aside on a plate.

Add the reduced-fat spread to the frying pan and let it melt. Add the onions and sprinkle over some salt. Cook over a medium heat for 5 minutes, until slightly softened, stirring so they don't burn. Stir in the balsamic vinegar and allow it to reduce slightly, then stir in the honey. Cook for a couple of minutes until the onions are glossy but still slightly crunchy. Set aside with the squash.

Spray the frying pan with some low-calorie cooking spray and arrange the squash neatly in the bottom of the pan. Sprinkle over the crumbled Greek-style salad cheese, then top with the cooked onion and spread out evenly. Place the disc of pastry on top of the onions and use a spoon to tuck the edges down between the side of the pan and the squash and onions.

Place in the oven and bake for 25–30 minutes, or follow the instructions on the puff pastry packet, until the pastry is crisp and golden brown.

Carefully remove the pan from the oven and allow the tarte to rest for 5 minutes. Take a knife and gently run it around the edge of the pastry to loosen it slightly.

Place a large plate on top of the pan, then carefully flip it over. Give it a gentle shake to release the tarte and slowly lift off the pan. Serve warm, with a mixed salad.

CHEESY HAM *and* LEEK PIE

⏱ 20 MINS   🍲 50 MINS   ✕ SERVES 4

PER SERVING:
508 KCAL /49G CARBS

SPECIAL EQUIPMENT
28cm (11in) shallow casserole dish with lid, suitable for oven and hob

low-calorie cooking spray
2 x 200g smoked gammon steaks, any visible fat removed and cut into 1.5cm (¾in)-thick strips
2 leeks, trimmed, rinsed and thinly sliced
400g floury potatoes, peeled and cut into 1.5cm (¾in) dice
2 tsp smoked sweet paprika
400ml skimmed milk
1 tbsp cornflour, mixed to a slurry with 1 tbsp water
120g reduced-fat spreadable cheese
80g reduced-fat mature Cheddar, grated
125g filo pastry
freshly ground black pepper

TO ACCOMPANY
75g mixed salad
  (+ 15 kcal per serving)

There are few meals more comforting than a hearty homemade pie, and this filo-topped Cheesy Ham and Leek Pie is no exception. The scrunched-up sheets of filo pastry bake until golden and crisp, for a lovely crunch that you can't resist digging into. We've added cubes of potato into the creamy ham and leek filling, to make sure every portion is really satisfying, without the need to use another pan.

Special Occasion

Spray the casserole dish with low-calorie cooking spray and place over a medium-high heat. Add the gammon and fry for 5 minutes until well sealed. Reduce the heat slightly, add the leeks and cook for a further 5 minutes until soft.

Add the potatoes and paprika and stir well. Pour in the milk and turn up the heat until it begins to boil. Reduce the heat to a simmer, then pour in the cornflour slurry and stir until thickened. Cover with the lid and simmer gently for 15–20 minutes, until the potatoes are soft but still holding their shape.

Preheat the oven to 200°C (fan 180°C/gas mark 6).

Turn off the hob and stir in the spreadable cheese and Cheddar until melted. Season with some pepper.

Take the filo pastry and spray each sheet liberally with low-calorie cooking spray.

Scrunch each sheet lightly and arrange over the top of the dish, tearing if necessary, to completely cover the top. Place in the oven and cook for about 20 minutes, or until the pastry topping is golden and crisp.

TIPS:

This pie is best served straight from the oven while the pastry is still crisp.

125g of filo is around half a pack. Buy it chilled, then wrap the leftover filo sheets thoroughly and freeze for future use.

SLOW COOKER FOCACCIA

🕐 **20 MINS**   🍲 **1 HR 30 MINS–2 HRS***   ✕ **SERVES 12**

*PLUS 30 MINS PROVING

PER SERVING:
169 KCAL /31G CARBS

SPECIAL EQUIPMENT
3.5-litre slow cooker

¼ tsp sea salt
1 tsp white granulated
  sweetener
7g fast-acting dried yeast
500g strong white bread
  flour, plus extra for dusting
300ml warm water
1 tbsp olive oil

FOR THE TOP
1 tbsp olive oil
2 tbsp fresh rosemary leaves,
  roughly chopped
2 garlic cloves, peeled and
  crushed
1 tsp sea salt

Sometimes the simplest flavours are the most delicious, and that's exactly why we've infused this dough with classic garlic, sea salt and rosemary. Once the bottom of your bread is lightly golden from slow-cooking, pop it under a hot grill for 5 minutes until browned on the top too. It's best enjoyed fluffy and warm!

Everyday Light ─────────────

Turn the slow cooker on low and put the lid on to preheat it. Put the salt, sweetener and yeast into a large bowl. Add the flour and mix. Make a well in the middle of the flour and pour in the warm water and ½ tablespoon of the olive oil. Mix with your hands, bringing it together into a sticky rough ball. Cover with a tea towel and leave in a warm place for 15 minutes.

Lightly dust your work surface with a little flour and tip out your dough. Knead for 5 minutes until the dough forms a smooth ball.

Turn the slow cooker off. Add the remaining ½ tablespoon of olive oil to the pot of the slow cooker and rub into the bottom and sides of the bowl. Add your dough to the slow cooker and spread it out to cover the bottom of the pot. Cover with the lid and leave to prove for 30 minutes.

In a small bowl, combine the oil, rosemary and garlic for the top. The dough should have risen and doubled in size. Remove the slow cooker lid and make dimples on the surface of the dough using your fingers. You might find it easier to coat your fingertips in a little flour. Pour over the rosemary mixture and lightly rub into the surface of the dough. Sprinkle over the sea salt.

Switch the slow cooker on high. Cover with the lid and cook on high for 1½–2 hours. The surface of the dough should be set and firm. Try not to remove the lid while cooking as this will reduce the temperature in the slow cooker.

Carefully remove the focaccia from the slow cooker. The edges and bottom should be lightly golden brown. Place the focaccia onto a baking tray and pop under a preheated grill for 4–5 minutes, until the top is lightly golden brown and crispy. Slice and serve.

BAKES *and* ROASTS

SWEET TREATS

VEGGIE

VEGAN

USE VEGAN
REDUCED-FAT
SPREAD

FREEZE
ME

BATCH
COOK

DAIRY
FREE

USE DF REDUCED-
FAT SPREAD

SUMMER BERRY BETTY

🕐 **10 MINS**   🍲 **25 MINS'**   ✕ **SERVES 4**

'PLUS 10 MINS COOLING

PER SERVING:
371 KCAL /73G CARBS

SPECIAL EQUIPMENT
**Large ovenproof dish
(about 18 x 27cm/7 x 10½in)**

400g fresh strawberries,
  stalks removed and halved
300g fresh raspberries
200g fresh blueberries
150g fresh blackberries
100g white granulated
  sweetener or granulated sugar
3 tbsp cornflour
3 tbsp fresh orange juice

FOR THE TOPPING
50g panko breadcrumbs
20g ground almonds
20g white granulated
  sweetener or granulated sugar
25g reduced-fat spread, melted

TO ACCOMPANY *(optional)*
12.5g swirl of reduced-fat
  aerosol cream (+ 24 kcal per
  serving)

This fruity, nutty, crunchy-topped pudding is gorgeous with a swirl of reduced-fat aerosol cream. We use a medley of berries for the filling and bake them until their juices create an irresistibly sweet syrup. Traditional versions of this hearty pud usually involve drying out fresh breadcrumbs in the oven, to make them crispy. Our method is far simpler, thanks to the magic of panko breadcrumbs! A dash of zesty orange juice and mellow ground almonds add an extra boost of flavour in every satisfying, golden-topped bite.

Special Occasion

Preheat the oven to 220°C (fan 200°C/gas mark 7).

Put the strawberries, raspberries, blueberries, blackberries, sweetener or sugar, cornflour and orange juice in a large bowl and mix until evenly coated.

Place the fruit in the ovenproof dish and spread it out evenly.

Put the panko breadcrumbs, ground almonds and sweetener or sugar in a small bowl and stir until evenly mixed. Add the melted reduced-fat spread and stir until the breadcrumb mixture is well coated.

Sprinkle the breadcrumb mixture over the fruit and place the dish on a baking tray. Bake in the oven for 20–25 minutes, until the fruit is soft, the juices are syrupy and bubbling, and the top is crisp and golden brown.

Remove from the oven. The fruit filling will be very hot so allow it to cool for 10 minutes before serving. Serve alone or with a swirl of aerosol cream.

The pudding will keep in the fridge for up to 3 days. Reheating in a moderate oven will result in a crispier breadcrumb topping.

TIPS:

Make sure to use white granulated sweetener with the same weight, texture and sweetness as sugar – not the powdered type.

Add the breadcrumb topping to the fruit just before baking so it stays crisp and dry.

VEGGIE

VEGAN

USE VEGAN
REDUCED-FAT
SPREAD

**FREEZE
ME**

**BATCH
COOK**

**DAIRY
FREE**

USE DF REDUCED-
FAT SPREAD

**GLUTEN
FREE**

USE GF FLOUR
AND OATS

SLOW COOKER PEACH AND RASPBERRY CRUMBLE

🕐 **10 MINS**   🍲 **3 HRS**   ✕ **SERVES 6**

PER SERVING:
184 KCAL /30G CARBS

SPECIAL EQUIPMENT
3.5-litre slow cooker

2 x 400g tins peach slices in
   juice, drained
150g raspberries, fresh or frozen
1–2 tbsp granulated sweetener
   (or granulated sugar),
   according to taste

FOR THE CRUMBLE MIX
50g plain flour
50g reduced-fat spread
50g oats
2 tbsp granulated sweetener

This lazy pud is our favourite kind of recipe! It takes less than 10 minutes to prepare the ingredients, then you can walk away and let your slow cooker do the rest of the work. Sweet, juicy tinned peaches steal the show in this comforting dessert, so there's no need for any peeling or slicing. Fresh or frozen raspberries add a little bit of tartness, then everything is crowned with a golden oaty topping that's a cross between a crumble and a cobbler.

Everyday Light ────────────

Put the peaches and raspberries in the slow cooker pot and stir in the granulated sweetener or sugar.

Put the flour in a mixing bowl and add the reduced-fat spread. Using the tips of your fingers, rub the spread into the flour, until it comes together and resembles breadcrumbs. Stir in the oats and granulated sweetener.

Sprinkle the crumble mix evenly over the fruit. Lay a clean tea towel over the top of the slow cooker pot and cover with the lid. The tea towel will absorb any condensation and prevent the crumble becoming soggy. Cook on high for 2½ hours. Turn the slow cooker down to low and remove the lid and tea towel. Cook, uncovered, for a further 30 minutes. Serve!

IF YOU DON'T HAVE A SLOW COOKER
Alternatively, cook this crumble in the oven. Preheat the oven to 180°C (fan 160°C/gas mark 4). Assemble the crumble in an ovenproof dish approximately 27 x 18cm (10½ x 7in) in size. Bake for 45 minutes until the topping is golden and crisp. This will give a crispier crumble .

VEGGIE

VEGAN

USE VEGAN
YOGHURT
AND CREAM
ALTERNATIVE

DAIRY
FREE

USE DF YOGHURT
AND CREAM
ALTERNATIVE

BISCOFF MOUSSE

 5 MINS   **30 SECS***   ✕ **SERVES 4**

*PLUS 30 MINS CHILLING

PER SERVING:
234 KCAL / 16G CARBS

SPECIAL EQUIPMENT
**4 x 125ml ramekin dishes,
electric hand whisk**

100ml light double cream
  alternative
80g smooth Biscoff spread
100g fat-free Greek-style
  yoghurt
1 tsp vanilla extract
½ Biscoff biscuit, crumbled

Perfectly portioned for an after-dinner treat, these gorgeous Biscoff Mousse pots are light, airy and unbelievably creamy all at the same time. Proving that nothing is ever off the menu, our slimming-friendly recipe uses a low-fat double cream alternative and fat-free Greek-style yoghurt to get that velvety texture without all the calories. A sprinkle of crumbled Biscoff biscuits is a dreamy finishing touch, adding an irresistible crunch.

Weekly Indulgence

Pour the light double cream alternative into a medium mixing bowl and whisk using an electric hand whisk, on high speed, for about 2 minutes until soft peaks are formed. Take care not to over-whisk the cream alternative otherwise it will become too stiff to fold in the remaining ingredients.

Put the Biscoff spread in a small microwaveable bowl and microwave in small bursts until melted and completely smooth and runny. Alternatively, place the small bowl in a slightly larger heatproof bowl containing boiling water and stir for about 2 minutes.

Add the yoghurt, melted Biscoff spread and vanilla extract to the bowl with the whipped cream alternative and fold in gently using a rubber spatula or large metal spoon until completely combined. Take care not to knock the air out of the mixture.

Divide among the ramekin dishes and sprinkle the Biscoff biscuit crumbs on top. Chill for about 30 minutes then serve.

TRIPLE CHOCOLATE CAKE

🕐 **10 MINS**   🍲 **25 MINS**   ✕ **MAKES 16 SQUARES**

PER SQUARE:
114 KCAL /13G CARBS

SPECIAL EQUIPMENT
20 x 22cm (8 x 8 ½ in)
ovenproof dish, electric whisk
(useful but not essential)

100g self-raising flour
100g reduced-fat spread, plus
   a little extra for greasing
50g white granulated
   sweetener
50g caster sugar
½ tsp baking powder
15g cocoa powder
2 medium eggs
1 tsp vanilla extract
15g dark chocolate chips
15g white chocolate chips
15g milk chocolate chips

FOR THE TOP
2 tsp low-calorie chocolate
   flavour syrup

TIP:

To freeze, pack into a
freezerproof container
layered between sheets
of non-stick baking
paper and follow
standard guidelines for
defrosting.

Drizzle with low-calorie
chocolate syrup after
defrosting.

You'll find white, dark and milk chocolate chips in this
indulgent-tasting baked treat! The scrumptious sponge is
made slimming friendly by using reduced-fat spread and
white granulated sweetener. You'll want to make sure that
your sweetener has the same weight and texture as sugar,
so that your chocolatey, squidgy squares are as light as
possible. Once your cake has risen and is springy to touch,
that's your cue to serve with a drizzle of chocolate syrup –
and a cup of tea, of course!

Everyday Light ────────────────────────

Preheat the oven to 180°C (fan 160°C/gas mark 4) and
grease the ovenproof dish well with a little reduced-fat
spread.

Put the flour, reduced-fat spread, granulated sweetener,
caster sugar, baking powder, cocoa powder, eggs and
vanilla extract in a medium mixing bowl and beat together
for 1–2 minutes with an electric whisk until light and creamy.

Alternatively, you can use a wooden spoon, but it will take
more effort.

Use a large metal spoon to gently fold in two thirds of the
chocolate chips, taking care not to knock out the air you
have incorporated. Use a rubber spatula to scrape the
mixture from the mixing bowl into the greased ovenproof
dish and level the surface with a knife, if needed. Scatter
the remaining chocolate chips on top.

Bake in the oven for 20–25 minutes, until risen and spongy.
To test if the sponge is ready, insert a small sharp knife into
the centre; when the sponge is cooked the knife will come
out clean. Leave the sponge in the dish to cool.

When the cake is cool, run a round-bladed knife around the
edge, cut into 16 squares and remove carefully from the dish.
Drizzle with low-calorie chocolate flavour syrup and serve.

The cake will keep in the fridge for up to 3 days.

VEGGIE

FREEZE
ME

WITHOUT THE
SYRUP DRIZZLE

BATCH
COOK

DAIRY
FREE

USE DF
CHOCOLATE
CHIPS AND DF
REDUCED-FAT
SPREAD

GLUTEN
FREE

USE GF FLOUR
AND BAKING
POWDER

SWEET TREATS

SLOW COOKER CHOCOLATE CHERRY CHEESECAKES

🕐 **20 MINS**   🍲 **1½ HRS***   ✕ **MAKES 4**

*PLUS 2 HRS CHILLING

PER SERVING:
261 KCAL /33G CARBS

SPECIAL EQUIPMENT
3.5-litre slow cooker, four
7.8 x 4.5cm (3 x 2in) ramekins

FOR THE BASE
6 Oreo biscuits (about 66g),
    crushed
15g reduced-fat spread, melted

FOR THE FILLING
100g reduced-fat cream cheese
80g fat-free Greek-style
    yoghurt
1 medium egg
25g white granulated
    sweetener
2 tbsp unsweetened cocoa
    powder
½ tbsp cornflour
1 tsp vanilla extract
2 tbsp light syrup from the
    tinned cherries
95g tinned cherries in light
    syrup, sliced in half

TO DECORATE
5g dark chocolate,
    finely grated
4 fresh cherries

TIP:
You can use a
vegetable peeler to
grate your chocolate .

Chances are you've never made cheesecake in a slow cooker before but, trust us, it works a treat! These delightful Chocolate Cherry Cheesecakes are the definition of baking made easy. We've made the super simple, crunchy base from crushed-up Oreo biscuits, which make for a scrumptious pairing with juicy-sweet tinned cherries. A silky, indulgent-tasting dessert, you'd never guess we've used reduced-fat ingredients and sweetener for our cheesecake mixture. Don't forget to top them with dark chocolate shavings and a fresh cherry to make them even more impressive!

Weekly Indulgence

Combine the crushed biscuits with the melted reduced-fat spread in a bowl. Press into the base of 4 ramekins.

In a mixing bowl, beat together the cream cheese, Greek yoghurt, egg, sweetener, cocoa, cornflour, vanilla extract and fruit syrup using a wooden spoon, until smooth.

Arrange the tinned cherries on top of the biscuit layer in the ramekins and pour the cheesecake mixture evenly over each.

Place the ramekins into the slow cooker pot and carefully pour 300ml cold water into the pot around the ramekins, making sure the water doesn't pour into the mixture. Lay a tea towel over the top of the slow cooker then place the lid on top of the towel. Cook on low for 1½ hours. The mixture should be set with a slight wobble.

Leave the ramekins in the slow cooker until cool enough to handle, then lift out of the slow cooker and leave to cool at room temperature for an hour. Place into the fridge for an hour, or until ready to serve.

Top each cheesecake with some grated chocolate and a fresh cherry. Serve.

SWEET TREATS

VEGGIE

FREEZE ME

BATCH COOK

DAIRY FREE

USE DF SPREAD, MILK AND CHOCOLATE

SLOW COOKER SELF-SAUCING CHOCOLATE PUDDING

🕐 **10 MINS**   🍲 **1 HR 45 MINS**   ✕ **SERVES 8**

PER SERVING:
341 KCAL /43G CARBS

SPECIAL EQUIPMENT
3.5-litre slow cooker, electric whisk

250g self-raising flour
100g reduced-fat spread, plus a little extra for greasing
40g caster sugar
40g white granulated sweetener
30g cocoa powder
3 medium eggs
150ml skimmed milk
80g milk chocolate chips

FOR THE TOP
500ml boiling water
20g cocoa powder
20g white granulated sweetener

As it slow cooks, this easy dessert creates its own rich, chocolatey sauce, so there's no need to rustle up a jug of custard to serve with it. Almost too good to share, it takes no time at all to mix together the ingredients, and then it's all in the safe hands of your slow cooker. Don't be scared to pour the boiling water and cocoa mixture over the batter! Trust the process and you'll be rewarded with the ultimate chocolate pudding.

Special Occasion

Grease the pot of the slow cooker with a little reduced-fat spread.

Put the flour, spread, sugar, sweetener, cocoa, eggs and milk in a mixing bowl. Whisk with an electric whisk for about 2 minutes until creamy.

Pour into the dish of the slow cooker and sprinkle over the chocolate chips.

In a jug, combine the boiling water with the cocoa and sweetener and mix until dissolved.

Pour over the cake batter in the slow cooker. It may feel wrong to pour boiling water over the chocolate sponge mixture, but trust the process! Cover with the lid, set the slow cooker to high and cook for 1 hour 45 minutes.

The cake should be firm and set on the top. If it's not, re-cover and cook for a further 30 minutes. Serve.

TIP:
We used 80g milk chocolate chips, but you could use chopped milk chocolate or dark chocolate instead!

CHOCOLATE ORANGE RICE PUDDING

⏱ **5 MINS** 🍲 **35 MINS** ✕ **SERVES 4**

VEGGIE

VEGAN

USE PLANT-BASED CHOCOLATE ORANGE BAR

FREEZE ME

BATCH COOK

DAIRY FREE

USE PLANT-BASED CHOCOLATE ORANGE BAR

GLUTEN FREE

PER SERVING:
218 KCAL / 37G CARBS

100g short-grain pudding rice
800ml unsweetened almond milk
1 tbsp cocoa powder
finely grated zest of 1 orange
1 tsp vanilla extract
50g orange-flavoured chocolate, roughly chopped
1–2 tbsp granulated sweetener
2 tsp low-calorie chocolate-flavoured syrup

Comfort by the spoonful, you won't believe how simple it is to make this chocolate-loaded rice pudding. Luxuriously creamy for far fewer calories than you'd expect, our recipe simmers silky almond milk and cocoa powder with pudding rice, until fluffy. We've used fresh orange zest and Terry's Chocolate Orange segments for extra indulgence, but you can melt in any orange-flavoured chocolate bar you like – it'll still be delicious!

Weekly Indulgence

Put the rice, almond milk, cocoa powder, orange zest and vanilla extract in a saucepan and whisk well.

Place over a medium-high heat until just boiling (keep an eye on it as it can boil over quickly), then reduce the heat and simmer for 30–35 minutes, stirring occasionally, until the rice is tender and the pudding is thick and creamy.

Remove from the heat and stir in the chopped chocolate orange, until melted. Taste and add 1–2 tablespoons of sweetener, to taste.

Spoon into bowls and drizzle a little chocolate syrup on each. Serve!

The pudding will keep in the fridge for up to 3 days.

TIP:
If you are reheating after freezing and defrosting, the pudding may have thickened up. Use a splash of almond milk to thin it down while reheating.

VEGGIE

FREEZE ME

BATCH COOK

DAIRY FREE

USE DF SPREAD

SLOW COOKER STEAMED BANANA SPONGE

🕐 **5 MINS**   🍲 **2 HRS**   ✕ **SERVES 8**

PER SERVING:
207 KCAL /28G CARBS

SPECIAL EQUIPMENT
3.5-litre slow cooker, 2-pint pudding basin, electric whisk (*optional*)

2 small, ripe bananas, peeled and mashed
100g self-raising flour
100g reduced-fat spread, plus a little extra for greasing
75g granulated sweetener
2 medium eggs
1 tsp vanilla extract
½ tsp baking powder
3 tbsp maple syrup

TO ACCOMPANY
12.5g swirl of reduced-fat aerosol cream (+ 24 kcal per serving)

A slow cooker is ideal for making soft, spongy steamed puddings that never dry out! For this fruity treat, we've made a simple banana sponge and topped it with maple syrup for an extra level of sweetness. The syrup soaks into the sponge, keeping it moist yet light, at just 167 calories per slice. Serve it with a swirl of aerosol cream or a dollop of low-calorie custard and it's sure to be your new favourite dessert.

Weekly Indulgence

Grease the pudding basin with a little reduced-fat spread. Put all the ingredients, except the maple syrup, in a mixing bowl and beat together until thoroughly mixed. Using an electric whisk will make this easier, but you can also use a spatula and some elbow grease.

Pour the mix into the greased pudding basin and cover the top with a piece of foil, crimping the foil around the edges to loosely seal.

Pour 2.5cm (1in) of boiling water into the slow cooker pot and turn to high. Carefully place the pudding basin into the slow cooker pot, cover with the lid and cook for 2 hours, or until a skewer inserted into the centre of the pudding comes out clean.

Use a round-bladed knife to loosen the sides of the pudding, then turn out the basin onto a plate and gently shake to remove the pudding.

Drizzle over the maple syrup, before cutting into 8 portions and serving with your chosen accompaniment .

IF YOU DON'T HAVE A SLOW COOKER
Alternatively, you can cook this in the microwave. Use a microwave-safe pudding basin. Cover with cling film, pierce the top and microwave on high for 2–3 minutes, until risen and a skewer inserted into the centre comes out clean. This is a quicker way to cook the pudding but may result in a denser sponge.

TIP:
Make sure to use white granulated sweetener with the same weight, texture and sweetness as sugar – not the powdered type.

SWEET TREATS

SLOW COOKER GIANT COOKIE

🕐 **10 MINS**　　🍲 **1½–2 HRS**　　✕ **SERVES 8**

PER SERVING:
293 KCAL /40G CARBS

SPECIAL EQUIPMENT
3.5-litre slow cooker

120g reduced-fat spread,
　plus a little extra for greasing
70g caster sugar
70g brown granulated
　sweetener
1 medium egg
1 tsp vanilla extract
200g plain flour
½ tsp bicarbonate of soda
pinch of salt
60g chocolate chips (we used
　a mixture of milk, dark and
　white)

TO ACCOMPANY *(optional)*
100g low-calorie vanilla ice
　cream (+ 163 kcal per serving)

TIPS:

We used brown granulated
sweetener, but white granulated
sweetener will be fine too.

We used a mixture of milk, dark
and white chocolate chips, but
if you prefer you could use all
of the same or 60g chopped
chocolate instead.

If freezing, once cool, divide into
portions and freeze in a suitable
container. Defrost overnight in
the fridge, cover and microwave
for 2 minutes until piping hot.

Imagine how incredible your kitchen will smell while this Slow Cooker Giant Cookie is busy baking away! We've packed our quick-to-make cookie dough with plenty of chocolate chips, which get gloriously gooey and melty as it bakes. When it's time to lift off the lid, the supersize cookie should be squidgy and soft, ready to slice and serve warm, with a scoop of your favourite ice cream. Psst… if you fancy a double whammy of chocolate indulgence, pour yourself a mug of our Slow Cooker Hot Chocolate!

Weekly Indulgence

Grease the pot of a slow cooker with a little reduced-fat spread. Line the bottom of the slow cooker pot with two strips of baking paper, overlapped in a cross shape.

Put the reduced-fat spread, caster sugar and sweetener in a mixing bowl and beat with a wooden spoon until combined and creamy. Add the egg and vanilla and mix again. Add the flour, bicarbonate of soda and salt and mix until you have a smooth, sticky dough. It will be a lot wetter than a usual rollable cookie dough, but don't worry.

Fold in the chocolate chips. Scrape the cookie dough into the slow cooker pot and roughly smooth it out with the back of a spoon. Cover with the lid and cook on high for 1½–2 hours. This is more of a soft-style cookie than a crispy one, so it will be quite soft (but not raw) when cooked. Serve on its own or with a scoop of ice cream.

VEGGIE

USE VEGGIE
FOOD
COLOURING

**DAIRY
FREE**

**GLUTEN
FREE**

CRANBERRY POACHED PEARS

🕐 **5 MINS**   🍲 **50 MINS**   ✕ **SERVES 4**

PER SERVING:
221 KCAL / 52G CARBS

800ml cranberry juice drink
2 tbsp clear honey
5g orange peel, all white pith removed and cut into fine strips
small pinch of ground cinnamon
4 whole cloves
a few drops of red food colouring *(optional)*
4 medium pears, peeled and stalks left on

TO ACCOMPANY *(optional)*
1 tbsp (45g) fat-free Greek-style yoghurt (+ 26 kcal per tablespoon serving)

Christmas cheer in a bowl, these deliciously rosy pears come brimming with festive flavours. Sweet, fruity and lightly spiced with cinnamon and cloves, we've also kept the aromas merry and bright with sweet cranberry juice and zingy orange zest. The perfect low-calorie pudding for when you're looking to round-off a heavy, wintery dinner, they'll also go down a treat with an added dollop of fat-free Greek yoghurt...or a glass of mulled wine!

Weekly Indulgence

Place the cranberry juice drink, honey, orange peel, cinnamon, cloves and red food colouring (if using) in a small saucepan. The saucepan needs to be small and deep enough for the pears to be just submerged in the liquid.

Place the saucepan over a medium heat and bring to the boil, then simmer, uncovered, for 10 minutes to allow the flavours to develop and the orange peel to become tender.

Add the pears to the cooking syrup, placing them on their sides or standing them up, whichever is best to just submerge them. Simmer, uncovered, for about 20 minutes until tender, turning them once halfway through. Insert a small sharp knife into the pears to check if they are tender.

Depending on the ripeness of your pears, this may take a little more or less time, but take care not to overcook the pears, as they may become mushy.

When the pears are tender, remove them from the syrup with a large slotted spoon and place them in a serving dish. Remove the cloves from the cooking syrup and discard.

Continue to simmer the cooking syrup, uncovered, for 15–20 minutes, to reduce and concentrate the flavours. The syrup will remain thin – it's not supposed to thicken. You should be left with about 200ml of thin syrup.

Spoon the syrup over the poached pears and serve alone or with a dollop of fat-free Greek yoghurt. The dish will keep in the fridge for up to 3 days.

TIP:

Make sure to remove all traces of the white pith from the orange peel before using, otherwise it may make the cooking syrup bitter.

SWEET TREATS

MANGO *and* COCONUT BREAD PUDDING

🕐 **15 MINS***   🍲 **30 MINS**   ✕ **SERVES 4**

*PLUS 10 MINS RESTING

FREEZE ME

BATCH COOK

DAIRY FREE
USE PLANT-BASED REDUCED-FAT SPREAD

GLUTEN FREE
USE GF BREAD

PER SERVING:
217 KCAL /33G CARBS

SPECIAL EQUIPMENT
25 x 20cm (10 x 8in) ovenproof dish (or 1.5-litre capacity), stick blender

½ tsp reduced-fat spread
6 slices of Danish-style white bread, cut into cubes
1 ripe and ready mango, peeled and cut into small dice
1 tbsp unsweetened desiccated coconut
2 medium eggs
350ml plant-based coconut drink
1 tbsp granulated sweetener

FOR THE MANGO SAUCE
1 ripe and ready mango, peeled and roughly chopped
juice of ½ lime
2 tbsp plant-based coconut drink
1–2 tsp granulated sweetener

TIP:

The sauce can be frozen in ice cube trays. Reheat the pudding, loosely covered, in the microwave for 3–4 minutes. Reheat the sauce separately for a shorter time.

You don't want to miss this tropical twist on classic bread and butter pudding. It uses sweet, juicy mango and creamy coconut, infusing the bread slices with exotic flavours, and is topped off with a moreish mango sauce. To cut calories, we blitz together eggs and a plant-based coconut drink with granulated sweetener to make a custard, then let that soak through the pudding, then it's ready to bake until gorgeous, golden and spongy. We love enjoying leftovers cold the next morning for breakfast!

Weekly Indulgence

Preheat the oven to 200°C (fan 180°C/gas mark 6) and lightly grease the ovenproof dish with the reduced-fat spread. Place the cubes of bread into the prepared dish. Scatter over the diced mango and half the desiccated coconut and gently stir so the fruit is evenly mixed in with the bread.

Beat together the eggs, plant-based coconut drink and the granulated sweetener. Pour the mix over the bread and mango and leave to rest for 10 minutes, to allow the custard to soak into the bread.

Sprinkle over the remaining desiccated coconut and bake in the oven for 30 minutes, until golden brown and springy to touch.

While the bread pudding cooks, make the sauce. Place the mango, lime juice and plant-based coconut drink in a bowl and use a stick blender to blitz everything into a smooth sauce (you can also use a small blender or food processor for this).

Taste the sauce and add granulated sweetener. How much you use will depend on your personal preference, and how sweet and ripe your mango is.

Remove the bread pudding from the oven and serve it in bowls, topped with the mango sauce. The pudding will keep in the fridge for up to 3 days.

SWEET TREATS

LEMON POSSET

🕐 **5 MINS**   🍲 **5 MINS***   ✕ **SERVES 4**

PLUS 1–2 HRS CHILLING*

PER SERVING:
251 KCAL / 9.2G CARBS

SPECIAL EQUIPMENT
4 x 100ml ramekins

270ml light double cream
   alternative
2½ tbsp white granulated
   sweetener
50ml freshly squeezed lemon
   juice (about the juice of
   1 large lemon)
1 tsp finely grated lemon zest
12 raspberries

Lemon Posset is one of those simple, timeless desserts that can be served at the end of just about any meal. Sweet and luxurious, our lower-calorie version swaps out full-fat cream for a lighter double cream alternative, and you can hardly tell the difference. When they're heated together, the cream reacts with the zingy lemon juice, making a zesty mixture that sets into a silky, thick dessert. Pop a few raspberries on the top (or a medley of berries!), grab a spoon and enjoy.

Weekly Indulgence

Pour the light double cream alternative into a small saucepan, add the sweetener and place over a medium-high heat. Bring to the boil, stirring until the sweetener has dissolved (be careful as it can quickly boil over), then reduce the heat to a simmer and cook for 5 minutes.

Stir in the lemon juice and zest, remove from the heat and let it stand for 5 minutes to cool slightly before pouring into the ramekins. Cover and chill for 1–2 hours, until set.

Decorate with fresh raspberries and serve.

The posset will keep in the fridge for up to 2 days.

TIPS:

We used raspberries, but blueberries or blackberries are fab too.

The small glass pots that famous readymade desserts are served in are an ideal size for this recipe.

This recipe will only work with double cream or a double cream alternative. Don't be tempted to use single cream to cut calories as it won't set.

SWEET TREATS

SLOW COOKER CINNAMON ROLL PUDDING

🕐 **15 MINS**　　🍲 **1½–3 HRS**　　✕ **SERVES 4**

PER SERVING:
278 KCAL /43G CARBS

SPECIAL EQUIPMENT
3.5-litre slow cooker

9 slices of lighter Danish white bread (about 225g total)
350ml skimmed milk
3 medium eggs
2 tsp ground cinnamon
2 tbsp white granulated sweetener
2 tsp vanilla extract

FOR THE ICING
2 tbsp icing sugar
2 tbsp reduced-fat cream cheese
1 tsp cold water

When bread and butter pudding and cinnamon rolls meet in the middle, you get this squishy, sweet, Slow Cooker Cinnamon Roll Pudding! We've said goodbye to all the faff of making a dough, and used lower-calorie bread for the base of this homely pud. It takes just a few ingredients to whip up the quick cinnamon-spiced custard that soaks into the rolled-up slices as it cooks. Whether you set the slow cooker on high or low, your patience will be rewarded once you've drizzled the syrupy-sweet cream cheese icing all over the top!

Weekly Indulgence

Cut the bread slices vertically into 3 strips. Roll the strips of bread up into spirals and place into the bottom of the pot of the slow cooker.

Put the milk, eggs, cinnamon, sweetener and vanilla in a jug or bowl and whisk together until smooth and combined. Pour the milk mixture evenly over the bread slices and leave to stand for 10 minutes.

Cover with the lid and cook on low for 2½–3 hours, or high for 1½ hours. The custard should be set, and the bread will be beginning to brown and crisp around the edges.

In a small bowl, combine the icing sugar with the cream cheese and water and mix until smooth. Drizzle over the pudding and serve.

IF YOU DON'T HAVE A SLOW COOKER
Alternatively, cook this pudding in the oven. Preheat the oven to 210°C (fan 190°C/gas mark 7). Arrange the bread swirls in the bottom of an ovenproof dish approximately 23 x 14cm (9 x 5½in) in size. Combine the milk, eggs, cinnamon, sweetener and vanilla and whisk until smooth. Pour the milk mixture over the bread and leave to stand for 10 minutes, then bake for 30 minutes until golden brown and the custard is set.

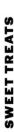
SWEET TREATS

VEGGIE
USE VEGGIE
MARSHMALLOWS

VEGAN
USE VEGAN
MILK, CREAM,
CHOCOLATE AND
MARSHMALLOWS

**DAIRY
FREE**
USE DF MILK
AND CREAM

**GLUTEN
FREE**

SLOW COOKER HOT CHOCOLATE

🕐 **10 MINS**   🍲 **2 HRS**   ✕ **SERVES 6**

PER SERVING:
239 KCAL /29G CARBS

SPECIAL EQUIPMENT
3.5-litre slow cooker

2 tbsp cocoa powder
2 tbsp white granulated
   sweetener
1 tsp vanilla extract
pinch of salt
1 litre skimmed milk
100ml light double cream
   alternative
80g milk chocolate chips
60g marshmallows, we used a
   mix of large and mini, to serve

Grab your favourite mug and get ready to sip our velvety, indulgent-tasting hot chocolate. Perfect when you're hosting friends and family, a big batch of this crowd-pleasing winter warmer will never go to waste! We've made a couple of slimming-friendly swaps to keep the calories down, but we couldn't resist throwing a good amount of chocolate chips into the pot for that extra bit of decadence. And don't worry...we haven't forgotten the marshmallows for the top!

Weekly Indulgence

Combine the cocoa powder, sweetener, vanilla and salt in a small jug or bowl. Add 4 tablespoons of the milk and mix until smooth.

Pour the remaining milk and the cream alternative into the pot of the slow cooker. Pour in the cocoa powder mixture and mix until fully combined. We used a balloon whisk to do this, but a wooden spoon works fine too.

Add the chocolate chips and cover with the lid. Set the slow cooker on low and cook for 1 hour.

Remove the lid and stir, making sure none of the chocolate chips have stuck to the bottom of the slow cooker. Re-cover with the lid and cook for a further hour.

Pour into mugs, top with the marshmallows and serve!

IF YOU DON'T HAVE A SLOW COOKER
Alternatively, cook this in a large saucepan. Follow the steps above, adding everything to the saucepan and covering with a lid. Simmer over a low heat for 30 minutes, stirring occasionally, until the chocolate chips have melted.

TIP:
You can swap the chocolate chips for chopped milk chocolate instead.

NUTRITIONAL INFO (PER SERVING)

SOUPS	ENERGY KJ/KCAL	FAT (G)	SATURATED FAT (G)	CARBS (G)	SUGAR (G)	FIBRE (G)	PROTEIN (G)
BUTTERNUT SQUASH AND ROCKET SOUP	440/105	5.2	2.4	11	5.7	2.7	2.5
UKRAINIAN-STYLE BORSCHT	806/191	2.2	0.4	29	19	7.6	9.9
CARROT AND LENTIL SOUP	390/93	2	0.3	12	6.7	5	3.8
MOROCCAN-STYLE SOUP	656/156	1.6	0.2	23	6.6	6.6	7.3
CREAMY BEAN SOUP	663/158	4.1	1.7	15	3.2	6.3	12
SLOW COOKER CHICKEN BROTH	1017/241	2.4	0.5	29	8.4	7.8	22
SMOKY CHICKEN AND CHORIZO SOUP	653/155	5.1	1.4	14	6.7	2	12
SWEET POTATO AND MISO SOUP	742/176	1.7	0.4	33	12	5.4	4.5
VEGETABLE CHOWDER	918/219	6.4	3.3	26	9.8	4.9	12
SLOW COOKER CHEESEBURGER SOUP	875/208	4.6	2.2	24	5.9	3.9	15
SLOW COOKED CHINESE-STYLE CHICKEN NOODLE SOUP	1384/328	3.7	0.8	39	13	7.9	30
SLOW COOKER SMOKY FISH SOUP	1042/247	5.3	0.9	22	10	7.7	23

STEWS and CASSEROLES	ENERGY KJ/KCAL	FAT (G)	SATURATED FAT (G)	CARBS (G)	SUGAR (G)	FIBRE (G)	PROTEIN (G)
HARISSA BEEF STEW	1196/284	8.1	2.8	22	13	5.9	27
LENTIL STEW WITH HERBY DUMPLINGS	1957/465	8.4	2.9	68	21	15	22
SPICY COD ONE-POT	1495/354	3.1	0.5	33	18	15	38
VEGGIE BLACK BEAN STEW	1618/385	9.5	6.7	50	23	18	16
ITALIAN SAUSAGE STEW	1862/442	8	2.7	59	20	13	26
HAM AND BEAN CASSEROLE	2890/685	5.9	1.4	72	11	31	71
PERSIAN-STYLE LAMB STEW	1785/424	12	4.3	40	21	8.8	34
BEEF AND HORSERADISH STEW	1681/400	11	2.9	36	16	9.1	35

STEWS and CASSEROLES	ENERGY KJ/KCAL	FAT (G)	SATURATED FAT (G)	CARBS (G)	SUGAR (G)	FIBRE (G)	PROTEIN (G)
SLOW COOKER PEPPERED BEEF WITH PASTA	1923/457	14	7.1	50	5.6	4	32
BEAN AND MUSHROOM BOURGUIGNON	1012/240	1.9	0.3	36	12	13	13
SLOW COOKER VEGETARIAN GOULASH	1402/333	2.2	0.4	49	21	19	18
SLOW COOKER VEGETARIAN WHITE CHILLI	1350/321	6.5	3	35	14	17	22
LAMB AND BARLEY CASSEROLE	1595/380	11	4.5	34	14	9.5	30
MEDITERRANEAN-STYLE CHICKEN STEW WITH FETA DUMPLINGS	2035/483	8.9	2.7	50	15	11	44
ONE-POT QUINOA CHILLI	1370/325	4.4	0.7	48	21	12	15
FULL ENGLISH CASSEROLE	1513/360	10	2.8	32	13	9	29
ONE-POT SAUSAGE BOLOGNESE	1817/431	7.4	2.3	59	19	10	24
SAUSAGE AND LENTIL STEW	1363/324	6.4	2	38	19	12	21
SLOW COOKER CREAMY SAUSAGE AND BEAN CASSEROLE	1458/347	9.2	4.1	37	9.7	8.7	24

FAKEAWAYS	ENERGY KJ/KCAL	FAT (G)	SATURATED FAT (G)	CARBS (G)	SUGAR (G)	FIBRE (G)	PROTEIN (G)
FRUITY CHICKEN CURRY	1428/339	8.4	3.5	26	22	3.8	37
KORAI-STYLE CHICKEN CURRY	1129/268	5.4	1.4	16	12	5.4	35
YELLOW PEA AND SWEET POTATO CURRY	1142/273	9.4	6.6	31	11	12	9.6
LAMB PASANDA	1680/402	22	7.5	15	9.5	3.5	34
CHILLI CHICKEN MASALA	835/198	2.6	0.6	11	8.6	3.9	29
ONE-POT CHICKEN TIKKI AND RICE	2102/497	6.5	2.3	65	17	5.9	41
TANDOORI-STYLE WHOLE CHICKEN WITH CUMIN-ROASTED VEGETABLES	2898/694	36	9.7	31	13	9.4	58
BRAZILIAN-STYLE PEANUT AND LIME CHICKEN CURRY	1083/257	7.2	2.1	7.3	5	2	39
THAI-STYLE BASIL TOFU STIRY-FRY	1401/333	11	1.8	33	7.5	5.2	23
SLOW COOKER SPICED COCONUT BEEF STEW	1543/368	14	7.9	13	8.2	2.8	47
GINGER MISO BEEF WITH NOODLES	1878/445	9.9	2.7	50	7.9	6	36

FAKEAWAYS	ENERGY KJ/KCAL	FAT (G)	SATURATED FAT (G)	CARBS (G)	SUGAR (G)	FIBRE (G)	PROTEIN (G)
SPICY VEGETABLE FRIED RICE	2242/536	25	4.8	53	13	9.6	20
CHINESE-STYLE STICKY PORK TRAYBAKE	1469/348	4.8	1.2	44	21	3.9	30
SLOW COOKER SWEET AND SOUR PORK NOODLES	2135/506	9.3	1.1	65	22	5.7	40
SLOW COOKER STICKY BBQ RIBS	987/236	12	4.6	12	11	0.8	18
SLOW COOKER CIDER PULLED PORK	632/150	4.4	1.4	4.8	2.3	0.5	21
CHILLI TORTILLA PIE	2299/547	15	6	50	10	13	45
CHEESEBURGER DIRTY RICE	1639/390	13	3.2	43	5.3	2.4	24
TOMATO AND PARMESAN RISOTTO	1802/426	6.8	3.6	71	11	3.8	16
SLOW COOKER SWEET POTATO AND FETA RISOTTO	1240/293	4.2	2.2	52	4.7	3	10
HARISSA CHICKEN MAC 'N' CHEESE	1893/450	12	6.1	45	11	4.1	38
CREAMY TOMATO, BACON AND SPINACH PASTA	2065/489	8	2.4	66	14	6.8	32
CHEESY BEEF RAGU	1567/372	8.7	4.2	35	14	5	35
SLOW COOKER CREAMY CHICKEN AND SWEETCORN PASTA	2106/499	9.6	4.3	57	11	7.2	41
CHICKEN, BACON AND LEEK MACARONI	2087/496	13	6.4	47	10	3.9	45
CHEESY SALMON AND LEEK ORZOTTO	1931/460	18	6.2	42	7.3	6.2	30
CREAMY CHICKEN LASAGNE	2025/481	14	7.9	41	7.9	4	46

BAKES and ROASTS	ENERGY KJ/KCAL	FAT (G)	SATURATED FAT (G)	CARBS (G)	SUGAR (G)	FIBRE (G)	PROTEIN (G)
SPANISH-STYLE CHICKEN TRAYBAKE	1496/355	9.5	2.6	26	10	6.1	38
CHEESY RAVIOLI LASAGNE	2442/584	31	18	32	11	3.2	40
TUNA, PEPPER AND POTATO BAKE	1478/351	8.6	4.6	37	11	6.3	28
SUMAC SALMON AND BULGUR WHEAT BAKE	2349/560	21	3.8	52	4.7	8.6	36
PEANUT CHICKEN AND SWEET POTATO TRAYBAKE	1883/447	11	3	38	14	7.9	45
CHEESY BUTTERNUT AND BACON ORZO	1765/419	10	4.7	53	12	7.5	26

BAKES *and* ROASTS	ENERGY KJ/KCAL	FAT (G)	SATURATED FAT (G)	CARBS (G)	SUGAR (G)	FIBRE (G)	PROTEIN (G)
CHICKEN, TOMATO AND POTATO BAKE	1621/384	6.9	3.4	35	12	6.5	41
SLOW COOKER CAJUN-STYLE CHICKEN THIGHS	1982/470	7.5	2	47	18	7.9	48
HARISSA PILAF	1841/438	12	1.3	65	6.2	6.1	14
SPICY PORK AND ROAST POTATOES	1500/357	11	1.6	28	5.6	6.1	34
CREAMY CHICKEN COBBLER	2212/528	13	4.6	60	11	8	37
PEA, POTATO AND ONION FRITTATA	1307/312	15	5	20	5.3	4.4	23
SLOW COOKER CHICKEN WITH APRICOTS	1754/416	7.9	1.8	39	22	9.7	43
CAJUN-STYLE CHICKEN ORZO	2084/493	7.6	1.8	59	12	8.5	43
MEDITERRANEAN-STYLE HALLOUMI BAKE	1669/398	13	7.1	37	16	11	25
SLOW COOKER STUFFED PEPPERS	966/230	6.4	1.9	26	14	7.9	12
LANCASHIRE HOTPOT	2352/560	17	7.1	51	16	11	45
PORK AND APPLE MEATLOAF WITH SAGE AND ONION ROASTIES	1665/394	6	1.8	40	11	7.1	41
HASSLEBACK POTATO AND BACON BAKE	1312/312	9.4	5	33	4.7	3.4	22
SLOW COOKER PORK POT ROAST	1602/380	8.8	2.7	35	11	6.4	38
PIZZA TART	1861/445	25	13	36	4.6	2.8	17
SMOKED HADDOCK, SPINACH AND GNOCCHI BAKE	1698/402	8.5	4.9	43	6.2	2.9	37
SUNDAY ROAST CHICKEN TRAYBAKE	1818/434	18	4.7	36	9.9	9.7	28
BAKED FETA, VEGETABLE AND COUSCOUS TRAYBAKE	2037/483	9.3	4.4	69	13	13	24
LAMB MEATBALL AND SWEET POTATO TRAYBAKE	1397/333	12	5.3	28	14	5.1	25
BUTTERNUT SQUASH AND RED ONION TARTE TATIN	1804/431	20	10	53	12	3.9	9.3
CHEESY HAM AND LEEK PIE	2137/508	15	7	49	11	5.4	42
SLOW COOKER FOCACCIA	713/169	2.6	0.4	31	0.5	1.6	5

SWEET TREATS	ENERGY KJ/KCAL	FAT (G)	SATURATED FAT (G)	CARBS (G)	SUGAR (G)	FIBRE (G)	PROTEIN (G)
SUMMER BERRY BETTY	1554/371	9.1	2.2	73	18	9.7	4.3
SLOW COOKER PEACH AND RASPBERRY CRUMBLE	772/184	7	2.2	30	8.7	2.5	2.4
BISCOFF MOUSSE	974/234	17	7	16	11	0	4
TRIPLE CHOCOLATE CAKE	474/114	6.4	2.3	13	5.1	0.6	1.9
SLOW COOKER CHOCOLATE CHERRY CHEESECAKES	1095/261	11	4.9	33	19	1.8	9.5
SLOW COOKER SELF-SAUCING CHOCOLATE PUDDING	1428/341	16	6	43	12	3.2	8.4
CHOCOLATE ORANGE RICE PUDDING	914/218	6.4	2.6	37	8.8	1.6	4.4
SLOW COOKER STEAMED BANANA SPONGE	866/207	11	3.5	28	8.7	0.8	3.3
SLOW COOKER GIANT COOKIE	1226/293	14	5.2	40	13	1	3.6
CRANBERRY POACHED PEARS	937/221	0	0	52	50	4.6	0.6
MANGO AND COCONUT BREAD PUDDING	913/217	6.5	3	33	14	2.5	7.6
LEMON POSSET	1036/251	24	14	9.2	3.4	0.6	1.7
SLOW COOKER CINNAMON ROLL PUDDING	1171/278	5.5	1.8	43	11	1.8	15
SLOW COOKER HOT CHOCOLATE	1002/239	11	5.9	29	23	0.5	7.8

NUTRITIONAL INFO

INDEX

Page references in **bold** indicate images.

INDEX

ACKNOWLEDGEMENTS

We owe many thank yous to many people who have worked so hard to bring this book together. Without these people, there would be no book. We deeply appreciate you all and can't thank you enough for the time and effort you put into making this book something we are immensely proud of.

We want to say a huge thank you firstly, to all of our followers on social media and all those who continue to make our recipes and let us know what you want next! We're so proud that Pinch of Nom has helped, and continues to help, so many people.

Thank you to our publisher Lizzy Gray. To Katy Denny, Cara Waudby-Tolley, Martha Burley, Bríd Enright, Jodie Mullish, Annie Rose, Sarah Badhan, Amy Winchester and the rest of the team at Bluebird for helping us create this book and continuing to believe in Pinch of Nom throughout our journey. Major thanks also to our agent Clare Hulton for your unwavering support and guidance.

To Ellis Parrinder for the amazing photos and to Kate Wesson and Max Robinson for making our food look so, so good. Thanks also to Tegan Ridgway and Kristine Jakobsson for all your assistance. Big thanks go out to Beth Free, Emma Wells and Nikki Dupin at Nic & Lou for making this book so beautiful!

We also want to thank our friends and family who have made this book possible. A very big thank you to Dr Hannah Cowan, Helen Child Villiers, Katie McKenna, Emma & Nicola Brooks and Kirsty Rogers. Your support has meant the world.

Special thanks go to Katie Mitchell and Rosie Sparrow for the endless hours you've put into this and for working so hard to get things right!

A huge thank you to our wonderful team of recipe developers who work tirelessly to help us bring these recipes to life; Lisa Allinson, Sharon Fitzpatrick and Holly Levell.

Massive thanks also go to Sophie Fryer, Hannah Cutting, Nick Nicolaou, Ellie Drinkwater and Laura Valentine for your writing and marketing support. To Cate Meadows and Jacob Lathbury for your creative and visual genius.

Additional thanks to Matthew Maney, Jessica Molyneux, Rubi Bourne and Vince Bourne for supporting us and the business – we are so proud to work alongside you all.

To our wonderful moderators and online support team; thank you for all your hard work keeping the peace and for all your support.

Furry thanks to Mildred, Wanda, Ginger Cat and Freda for the daily moments of joy.

And finally... Huge thanks go to Paul Allinson for your support and advice. And to Cath Allinson who is never forgotten. #YNWA

First published 2024 by Bluebird
an imprint of Pan Macmillan
The Smithson, 6 Briset Street, London EC1M 5NR
EU representative: Macmillan Publishers Ireland Ltd, 1st Floor,
The Liffey Trust Centre, 117–126 Sheriff Street Upper,
Dublin 1, D01 YC43

Associated companies throughout the world
www.panmacmillan.com

ISBN 978-1-5290-7948-7

1 3 5 7 9 8 6 4 2
A CIP catalogue record for this book is available from the British Library.
Printed and bound in China

Art Direction & Design Nikki Dupin, Emma Wells and Beth Free, Studio Nic&Lou
Illustration Shutterstock / Beth Free
Photography Ellis Parrinder
Food Styling Kate Wesson, Kristine Jakobssen, Tegan Ridgway
Prop Styling Max Robinson

Visit www.panmacmillan.com to read more about all our books
and to buy them. You will also find features, author interviews and
news of any author events, and you can sign up for e-newsletters
so that you're always first to hear about our new releases.